# Awaken the Dream

Indiana Tuggle

Dream Big and Watch God!

Indiana Tuggle

Cover design by K.E. Printing & Graphics, Memphis, TN.

Edited by Zipporah Williams, Memphis, TN.

Printed in the United States of America

# Dedication

*This devotional is dedicated to those who have a dream. To those who acknowledge the voice of the Lord calling them to be greater and to do greater.*

*May this devotional serve as daily encouragement when your faith is tested and/ or you have grown weary in well-doing.*

# Table of Contents

# 1

# All We Need is the Word

*In the beginning was the Word, and the Word was with God, and the Word was God.*

*John 1:1*

Everything we need is in the word. How do we expect to draw closer to God or learn who He is and how to trust Him without reading the word? Praying alone does not develop a well-rounded relationship with God. It is two-way. Prayers sometime seem empty, full of random words, materialistic requests, and meaningless repetition (saying the same thing over and over) because we fail to add the word. When you consistently study the word, you don't run out of things to say to God. When you study the word, you learn that it's not all about you and start to pray for others more than yourself.

I remember asking God why I had lost my ability to speak in tongues. His response was simple, "because you have not added the word. I have not left you; you walk away from Me by not reading My word. If you don't commune with Me, how can I commune with you. You silence Me without the word. You put Me in a box." Reading the word provides knowledge and guidance, speaking the word sets the heaven and earth in motion. And the word became flesh among us. If things are not happening in your life it's because you have not spoken the word over it and to it. Speak to your mountain and it shall be moved.

God wants a more personal relationship with us. Set away quiet time to spend alone with Him. In the informational age we live in today, technology controls our lives. Pencil God into your schedule on your planner, add Him to your daily tasks or calendar on your smartphone, IPad or tablet. Don't allow the enemy to tell you, you need to read a chapter or two a day or you need to spend hours laid prostrate before the Lord. There is a time and place when those may be necessary. However God is looking for quality over quantity. Schedule a time and stick to it. It may began as 15-minutes and soon flourish into an hour. Bible CDs are also good for the long commute. I have even found that it diminishes my road rage. It's hard to be screaming and wagging your finger at the car beside you with the bible playing in the backdrop. God is waiting, don't wait until it's too late.

**PRAYER:** *Dear Heavenly Father, I come to you first and ask for your forgiveness in not putting you first. I ask that you strengthen me the more and show me how to incorporate more time with you into my day. I bind distractions now in the name of Jesus and know that each day I spend with you is more rewarding than the last. I also ask that you increase my faith, and show me how to apply and to use what I have learned in my everyday life and to bless others along the journey. In Jesus' name, Amen.*

**<u>Reflection & Reaction</u>**

Quiet time is a necessity:

Have you allowed distractions to make you miss spending time praying and reading the word?

In what ways can you devote more time with God into your daily schedule?

______________________________________________

______________________________________________

______________________________________________

______________________________________________

______________________________________________

______________________________________________

______________________________________________

______________________________________________

# 2

# Where is your Faith?

*Now if God so clothes the grass of the field, which today is, and tomorrow is thrown into the oven, will He not much more clothe you, O you of little faith? Therefore do not worry, saying, 'What shall we eat?' or 'What shall we drink?' or 'What shall we wear?' For after all these things the Gentiles seek. For your heavenly Father knows that you need all these things. But seek first the kingdom of God and His righteousness, and all these things shall be added to you.*

*Matthew 6: 30-33*

Where is your faith? Do you believe the word that is written in the bible or do you believe it applies to "lucky" people? God is not a liar and His word will not return to Him void. As Christians we need to stand on the word. Sometimes standing on the word may mean we have to stand alone. We may have to stand against the gossipers, the naysayers, the haters, the non-believers, etc. "O you of little faith" this does not mean your faith is not "big" enough. As my pastor pointed out in church one Sunday, this statement means "refusal to hear, believe, or trust God's word." True faith "knows" without a shadow of doubt or fear that God will perform His word in His perfect timing.

We spend too much time thinking about material possessions and financial hardships. What bill has to be paid, repairs to the house or car, what clothes to buy, what food to buy, or what we can and can't afford. Too much time and energy is spent thinking and worrying about things that are beyond our control. God is aware of our needs. He wants us to focus on His needs (fulfilling our purpose) and He will handle the rest. Believe it or not our needs and wants are small pebbles in His hand. We were created for a purpose and that purpose is far greater than our natural eyes can see.

We learn to trust God by focusing on kingdom needs rather than our own present circumstances and issues. God requires our time. As we give Him our time; He will reveal the steps to fulfilling our purpose. When you are frustrated, give Him your time. When you are worried, give Him your time. Remember God is able to do exceedingly and abundantly above all we can ask or think, according to the power that works in us! Trust requires patience, allow God to complete a work in you.

**PRAYER:** *Dear Lord. Thank you for your word resonating in my heart on today. Speak to my mind Lord, Speak to my thoughts. Help me to think on things that are lovely, kind, pure, and beneficial to the kingdom. Help me to remember that you are aware of all that concerns me and are ever mindful of my needs. Help me to spend more time in your word and give me a greater revelation of who you are, your faithfulness and your will for my life. In Jesus' name, Amen.*

## Reflection & Reaction

What cares or worries have you allowed to distract you from the things of God?

Instead of worrying, write your concerns down, instead of contemplating them over and over in your head begin thanking God for working it out in your favor.

______________________________________________

______________________________________________

______________________________________________

______________________________________________

______________________________________________

______________________________________________

______________________________________________

______________________________________________

______________________________________________

______________________________________________

______________________________________________

______________________________________________

______________________________________________

# 3

# In Whom Do You Place Your Hope?

*Now hope does not disappoint, because the love of God has been poured out in our hearts by the Holy Spirit who was given to us.*

*Romans 5: 5*

If hope does not disappoint, then disappointment comes when hope is misguided or misdirected. Disappointment is then a result of placing hope in the wrong one. We put hope in men, they disappointed us. We put hope in ourselves and our own abilities, we were disappointed. Why? A sinful nature cannot instill hope because of pleasure seeking. Re-direct. Place your hope in Christ, the Creator rather than the created. Seek to please Him. When God is part of the thought process for every decision, every step, you can't go wrong, if you wait on His answer.

Hope is belief in what you cannot see. There is no hope without God. Because He is the only one who can see what you can't. He is the only one that can lead you to it. Without Him life is disappointing and frustrating. Frustration is a result of trying to do on your own, what only God can do. Relax and let God be God in your life. Trust Him even when you don't understand. Trust Him even when the path is not clear. Your job is to study the word. Allow God complete control. He will not disappoint. Why continue to try to take the wheel when you don't know where you are going? Two people can't be in control, both cannot drive. One has to sit on the passenger side, rest and enjoy the ride. Take in the scenery, smell the roses! Remember the journey is just as important as the final destination.

**PRAYER:** *Dear Father. Thank you for this word on today. Strengthen me the more. Increase my faith in you Lord. Help me to place my faith in you the giver of hope. I thank you for deliverance now, in the name of Jesus, for my past hurts and disappointments. Help me to forgive those who have hurt me as you have forgiven me. Show me how to walk in your love and deliverance, for your word promised me beauty for ashes. In Jesus' name, Amen.*

**Reflection & Reaction**

What disappointments or past hurts have caused you to lose hope?

Release the pain, anger, and frustration and allow God to show you how to forgive.

# 4

# Made Righteous

*For I bear them witness that they have a zeal for God, but not according to knowledge. For they being ignorant of God's righteousness, and seeking to establish their own righteousness, have not submitted to the righteousness of God.*

*Romans 10: 2-3*

It is impossible to serve God according to the knowledge of man or worldly understanding. Serving God is not limited to obeying the 10 commandments. The understanding of God's righteousness, His character and unconditional love, requires personal relationship. The righteousness of God is love, trust, and forgiveness. Worldly knowledge says that when you mess up you are a bad Christian or fall out of God's grace. But the righteousness of God says repent, and it is because of His grace that we are forgiven and can continue on the journey He has set before you.

Guilt and shame causes us to stop, give up, and have a pity party. God's purpose for our lives does not change when you make a mistake. Your purpose was written in stone before birth with full knowledge of your mistakes along the way. The inability to accept forgiveness keeps us stagnant. Constant asking of forgiveness of the same thing over and over again, crucifies God over and over again. Believe in your heart the first time you ask and no others are necessary. Walk in the freedom of knowing you are forgiven.

God has work to do in the earth, your talents and gifts are needed to complete them. No longer allow condemnation to prevent you from reaching your highest potential. Remember the enemy's job is to steal, kill and destroy. He cannot destroy God physically but he tries to do so by hindering the thoughts and actions of God's people. The enemy knows who you are, that's why he is working so hard against you. Do you know who you are?

**PRAYER:** *Heavenly Father, I thank you that I am made righteous in you. I thank you for forgiving me and I ask that you help me to remember that there is no condemnation in you. Today I walk in fullness of joy knowing that you have forgiven me and I am covered by your grace. As I* *make strides to continue in this newness I thank you that you have not forgotten me and will continue your perfect will through to completion. In Jesus' name, Amen.*

**Reflection and Reaction**

What do you continually ask for forgiveness for?

Starting today, thank God for forgiving you and ask Him to show you how to walk in it!

# 5

# Redeemed in Christ

*Blessed be the God and Father of our Lord Jesus Christ, who has blessed us with every spiritual blessing in the heavenly places in Christ, just as He chose us in Him before the foundation of the world, that we should be holy and without blame before Him in love, having predestined us to adoption as sons by Jesus Christ to Himself, according to the good pleasure of His will, to the praise of the glory of His grace, by which He made us accepted in the Beloved. In Him we have redemption through His blood, the forgiveness of sins, according to the riches of His grace which He made to abound toward us in all wisdom and prudence, having made known to us the mystery of His will, according to His good pleasure which He purposed in Himself, that in the dispensation of the fullness of the times He might gather together in one all things in Christ, both which are in heaven and which are on earth in Him. In Him also we have obtained an inheritance, being predestined according to the purpose of Him who works all things according to the counsel of His will that we who first trusted in Christ should be to the praise of His glory. In Him you also trusted, after you heard the word of truth, the gospel of your salvation; in whom also, having believed, you were sealed with the Holy Spirit of promise, who is the guarantee of our inheritance until redemption of the purchased possession, to the praise of His glory.*

*Ephesians 1: 3-14*

You are Holy and without blame. He finds no fault in you. You are His adopted daughter. He chose you. You are accepted. He wants you. You are redeemed and forgiven. You are made new, your sins are forgotten. You have an inheritance. You have access to your blessings now. You are predestined. You were created with a purpose. You are sealed with a promise. God does not break promises. You are a purchased possession. You are of value to Him.

You are of value. God made you, He wanted you. Recognize who you are in God, not who you think you are (according to past hurts or hurtful words of others) or who you think you should be (according to un-accomplished goals or dreams). Money, material possession, or status does not define who you are. God defined who you were at creation. You are in His image.

You are the chosen of Christ. He chose you from the beginning. Accept His choice. Acknowledge the call, and allow Him to show you what He wants you to do. The inability to move forward is caused by the lack of knowledge in who you are. Movement is tied to identity. Allow God to show you who you are: who you are in Him and who He is in you.

When God looks at you, He sees Himself. You are who He says you are. Believe His words. Repeat His words, mediate on them daily. Joy comes in the celebration of His greatest creation…"YOU". Open your spiritual eyes look in the mirror of your soul. There you shall find God, the greatness of His power and the beauty of you as His creation. You have work to do. Stop allowing the enemy to tell you who you are and what you can't do.

**PRAYER:** *Dear God thank you for this word today. Open my spiritual eyes and help me to see myself as you see me. Saturate me with your love, and show me how to accept your love. In Jesus' name, Amen.*

## Reflection and Reaction

Who are you?

Do you know who you are: beyond the titles at home, work, etc.? You are holy. You are of value. You are the chosen one!

Ask God to show you who you are in Him!

# 6

# Thy Good & Faithful Servant

---

*His Lord said to him, "Well done, good and faithful servant, you have been faithful over a few things, I will make you ruler over many things. Enter into the joy of your Lord.*

*Matthew 25:23*

Your faithfulness is required to receive success. Your faithfulness is also required to receive joy. Joy is not a result of success, it is a result of God's faithfulness and promises to you. If you do what He called you to do, He promises joy. If you complete the task He assigned you to do, He promises joy. God is a God of order. With each step you take, greater is waiting. The next step is only revealed after the completion of the first.

Have faith in God and He will give you joy. Joy begins with knowing that following God is the right path. There are no wrong turns with God. There are no regrets with God. Your past or your future are not the source of your joy. Joy is available now, if you choose to follow God. However, patience is a prerequisite. Trust that in due season you shall reap, if you faint not.

Remember God is time, therefore it shall not run out before His promises are fulfilled. Give Him your time (reading the word and obeying His commands) and He will pause time for you. God is preparing you for your greater, the wait is for you.

***PRAYER:*** *Dear God, thank you for your faithfulness towards me. Help me to be faithful in reading and studying your word. Show me how to patiently wait for your power and plan to be revealed in my life. Thank you for your joy and peace, in knowing that you are always at work in my life. In Jesus' name, Amen.*

## Reflection and Reaction

Are you a good and faithful servant?

What immediate changes can you make today to improve your faithfulness to God and His plan for your life?

Do you show up, when you are supposed to show up?

Do you do what you say you are going to do?

Do you hold yourself to the same standard you hold others?

# 7

# Don't Lose Heart

*Therefore I ask that you do not lose heart at my tribulations for you which is your glory.*

*Ephesians 3: 13*

When times get tough, it's easy to throw a pity party. Why me? Well, God is saying why not you? Becoming a Christian does not make one above life. Life happens. God rains on the just and the unjust. But God is saying, don't despise what you went through, for it is that very thing that will exalt you among His people and qualify you for His use.

The fight is not just about you. You are fighting for others as well. Those who are still condemned by their past, living in fear, afraid to live, afraid to ask for help, and afraid to come to God. Those who don't even know they need help and have become content with mediocrity, pain, sadness, hopelessness, etc.

Our testimonies are proof of God's power to help us overcome, to be victorious, and to be happy. The world is depending on you. Your pain will produce fruit. We have to allow God to show us the way and not become bitter in the process. Bitterness can stunt your growth, cause you to become stagnant, or even make you stay in the fire a little while longer. Remember trials make you stronger. Instead of asking "why me," ask "what do you want me to learn from this" so that you may teach others.

***PRAYER:*** *Dear God. I thank you for loving me. For your word says those whom you love you chastise. Your word also said that tribulations produce patience. Though it may be difficult now, I thank you that you are right here with me. Help me to remember that all things work together for the good of those who love the Lord and are called according to your purpose. In Jesus' name, Amen.*

## Reflection and Reaction

What have you been through? What have you survived?

How can you use your testimony to help others?

What lessons have you learned?

# 8

# Watch What You Say

*Let no corrupt word proceed out of your mouth, but what is good for necessary edification, that it may impart grace to the hearers.*

*Ephesians 4: 29*

Not only should you watch what you say concerning others, but you must especially watch what you say concerning yourself. God is the "Great I Am". "I Am" is His name. Anytime you use "I Am" angels in heaven rise ready to complete the task that follows. When the task is negative, it is like crying wolf. It is a false calling and the angels return disappointed because you still don't understand who you are and the power you carry as God's namesake.

The angels are jealous of you. You are God in the Earth. Things happen at the sound of your voice. Life and death lies in the power of the tongue. You have the power to change today and tomorrow, beginning with how you speak concerning yourself.

Start making positive declarations. You were not created for mediocrity. Greatness is in you, because God is great in you. Don't allow the enemy to distort your self-worth. The blood and your acceptance of salvation makes you worthy.

Your worthiness is not based on your behavior past or present. Rather your worthiness is based on God's love for you and His plans of hope and abundance that He created you for, came to this Earth for and died on the cross for. Regardless of what yesterday or today looks like, tomorrow can and will be better once you make a decision to think differently and react differently. Change does not happen overnight, but change is inevitable with God as the head of your life. Take control of your thoughts, take control of the words you speak and use them to build yourself up rather than help the enemy tear you down. Allow the love of God to transform you in every area of your life. Speak positively and watch positivity seek you and overtake you.

**Daily Positive Confession**:

*"I am the righteousness of Christ. I am who He says I am. I can have what He says I can have. The more I trust Him, the more He will increase and I will decrease. Success is all over me. Each day that I choose to follow God, I am successful. Each day that I allow God to uncover His abilities in me, I am successful. Success is doing what God created me to do. Success is God's vision coming to pass in my life. Today I relinquish my own vision of what my life should be or should have been to the will of God. I am intelligent and talented. I have yet to see the capabilities God has placed in me. Rather than fear what is to come, I fear what will not become if I remain in fear. Lord have your way in me."*

**Reflection and Reaction**

What negative thoughts or words have you allowed to stop you from pursuing your dreams?

List positive affirmations and begin replacing the negativity today.

# 9

# Approval Seeking

*But when it pleased God, who separated me from my mother's womb and called me through His grace, to reveal His son in me, that I might preach Him among the Gentiles, I did not immediately confer with flesh and blood.*

*Galatians 1: 15-16*

Who are you conferring with? Man cannot confirm or deny what God has purposed. Stop waiting on recognition, confirmation from others, a pat on the back, or a cheering section to push you into your destiny and pursuing your dreams. Truth is there will probably be more against you than for you. However, don't take it personally. It's not about you. It's about what and who you represent.

Generally when a person starts changing, seeking a personal relationship with God and moving towards their purpose, it will cause either support or opposition/rebellion from those around them. Support will come from those who are secure and confident in whom they are. They will push you into better and will be inspired by your tenacity. Opposition or rebellion, on the other hand comes from those who are not sure who they are or are refusing to know or acknowledge God. These people fear exposure. Greatness either exposes greatness or uncovers weakness.

We also have to be careful conferring with self. The flesh is weak, lazy, and does not like to be pushed out of its comfort zone. Greatness requires one to step out into the unknown and reliance on God for guidance and support. Self seeks self-gratification, pleasure, and immediate rewards. Greatness takes time, wisdom, and planning. When God reveals your purpose, it is not up for discussion. He will give you the steps to make it happen. Don't focus on your weaknesses and talk yourself out of your destiny. Doing so will keep you stagnant. Years later you will be reminiscing over what could have been.

**PRAYER:** *Dear heavenly father, thank you for the gifts and talents you have placed in me. Thank you for choosing me. Help me to trust you with all my heart and not lean on my own understanding. In all my ways I will* *acknowledge you and you shall direct my paths. Help me to be patient and to carry out your plan with wisdom and humility. In Jesus' name, Amen.*

## Reflection and Reaction

Generally the confirmation or validation we seek, God has already spoken.

Who does God say you are?

What does God say you can do?

# 10

# Stop Looking Back

*For if I build again those things which I destroyed, I make myself a transgressor. For I through the law died to the law that I might live to God. I have been crucified with Christ; it is no longer I who live, but Christ lives in me; and the life which I now live in the flesh I live by faith in the Son of God, who loved me and gave Himself for me.*

*Galatians 2: 18-20*

If you keep looking back, you will stumble over what is ahead. We can't change the past, and constantly looking back does not change the future either. But it can slow you down, thus making your journey longer. If you are constantly dwelling in the past, you are not living in the present. Christ died so that we would not be condemned by our past, so why do we keep taking the Band-Aid off the wound? It's time to heal and move on.

Your testimony should be told with joy and gratefulness to the goodness of God not with regret and sadness over what could have been. If God allowed it to happen, He wants to use it for your good. Good cannot come from regret, anguish, and disappointment. God promised us sunshine after the rain. Remember you must look up to see the rainbow.

Moving on may require you to physically move on. Sometimes we surround ourselves with people from our past that are hindering our blessings. These people do not see the woman of God you have become. They serve as a constant reminder of who you used to be. Truth is until you walk away from these people you will not enter your destiny. Your forward progress is hindered by the leeches you have allowed in your life and refuse to let go. What God has for you is for you, you can't take others with you. God will not allow someone or something unworthy or undeserving to latch on to your blessings.

**PRAYER:** *Heavenly Father, thank you for the many blessing you have bestowed upon me. Thank you for surrounding me with loving and supportive friends and family. However open my spiritual eyes and help me to walk away from people and things that are hindering my blessings. Give me the strength to walk away. In Jesus' name, Amen.*

**Reflection and Reaction**

Decide today that you will walk away from people and things that remind you of your past and hinder the call God has placed on your life.

Do you need to physically leave or move out? If so pray and make your plan today.

Surround yourself with people who celebrate who you are today not those who serve as a constant reminder of who you used to be.

# 11

# Who Do You Trust?

*But then, indeed, when you did not know God, you served those which by nature are not gods. But now after you have known God, or rather are known by God, how is it that you turn again to the weak and beggarly elements, to which you desire again to be in bondage?*

*Galatians 4: 8-9*

Why are we so quick to trust man more than God? Man can tell us about a money making opportunity and we quickly believe, get sucked into a pyramid scheme and lose all of our hard earned money. Yet the Lord tells us we are heirs to the promises of Abraham and we are filled with doubt and question the how, when, and where. How did we so easily forget that it is God who gives us the power and ability to obtain wealth?

Why does God have to prove Himself? Why do we question what is directly in front of us? History does not lie. The bible is filled with stories and testimonies of the goodness and faithfulness of God, yet we still require more proof. God has brought us out of dire situations and circumstances in our own past, yet we still do not believe. Do we not believe that nothing is impossible with God?

We trust man at the word of others, sight unseen. God has shown us His power and love towards us by working miracles in our own lives, yet we still do not believe. Unbelief limits God. He cannot do anything in your life if you do not believe that He can. Our unbelief is shown by our actions and the words we speak. Nothingness and negativity cancel out the movement of God. If we want our lives to change, if we want God to use us according to His purpose, if we want to live a life more abundant as the word promised, we must gird up our faith and speak those things that be not as though they were.

**PRAYER:** *Dear Heavenly Father, thank you for all that you have done in my life. Help me to remember that all things are possible with you. Help me to remember that you are the same God yesterday, today and forever more. If you did it then you can do it now. Help me to remember that you are faithful and that you are not a man that you should lie. Help my unbelief, and help me to trust your word, In Jesus' name, Amen.*

**Reflection and Reaction**

Trustfulness is proven through previous acts.

What has God done in your past? Is He not the same God that can do it again?

# 12

# Pressing Forward

*Brethren, I do not count myself to have apprehended; but one thing I do, forgetting those things which are behind and reaching forward to those things which are ahead, I press toward the goal for the prize of the upward call of God in Christ Jesus.*

*Philippians 3: 13-14*

In order to receive what God has for you. You must make a decision, sooner rather than later, hopefully today. You must draw a line in the sand and not allow the past to take over your present. You must decide to not only let go of the past but to forget, reach forward, and press on.

To forget "those things which are behind" means to stop thinking or caring about the past. You are not your past. You are not condemned by what happened or what did not happen. Stop trying to change it. Stop trying to justify it. Stop throwing a pity party. Stop trying to collect from people who don't owe you. How long are you going to allow your need to wallow in yesterday to take over today? How much time do you need? While you are waiting, life is moving on, and your purpose is growing impatient.

In order to "reach forward to those things which are ahead," you must stretch out or extend your body to get it. It's not going to come to you. It requires effort on your part. God is not going to hand it to you on a silver platter. How bad do you want it? What are you willing to do to get it? Faith without works is dead. You have to give God something to work with.

To "press toward the goal," is to act upon through steady pushing or thrusting force exerted in contact. You must consistently press. Day and night. Your purpose is an "upward call," meaning the more you press the higher you will go. There is not a stopping point. There is not one particular goal you are striving for. Your purpose is ongoing, you don't stop until God calls you home. Forget the past, reach for your purpose, take hold of it and press toward the ultimate prize in Jesus: to hear "well done thy good and faithful servant, enter into the joy of the Lord."

**PRAYER**: *Dear Most precious Lord. Help me to forget the past. Thank you for your forgiveness and help me to forgive myself as well as others. Show me how to move on into the purpose you have created me for. In Jesus' name, Amen.*

**Reflection and Reaction**

What steps can you implement today to forget the past, reach for those things ahead, and press toward your goals?

What is God telling you to do to go beyond your comfort zone?

# 13

# What Are You Thinking?

*For as he thinks in his heart, so is he.*

*Proverbs: 23:7a*

Our thoughts become our words and our words become our actions. Do your thoughts counteract the word of God? If you think on something long enough, you will make it happen. This is why the bible tells us to think on things that are pure and lovely. If you think, you are not good enough or you are not strong enough to carry out God's plan for your life, then you are held captive by your thoughts and more than likely will never try or give up quickly.

Most people feel like they can't control their thoughts. Well that is a lie from the enemy. We control our thoughts by counteracting it with the truth. The inability to control your thoughts is because you do not spend time in the word. The job of the Holy Spirit is to guide us into all truths, if there is no word in you, then the Holy Spirit has no truth to bring up in times of need.

The book of Romans tells us to be not conformed to this world but to be transformed by the renewing of our mind. We cannot renew our mind without the word. Going to church on Sunday is not enough. We must know the word for ourselves. You shall have what you think. If you have nothing it is because you think nothing of yourself.

**PRAYER:** *Heavenly Father, thank you for your word. Show me how to take control of my thoughts. Help me to spend more time with you, reading and studying your word. And in doing so help me to think more like you. In Jesus' name, Amen.*

**Reflection and Reaction**

Take note of the thoughts you have toward yourself.

What does the word say?

To quiet your thoughts you must open your mouth and speak to it!

# 14

# Examine Yourself, Check Your Motives

*But those who desire to be rich fall into temptation and a snare, and into many foolish and harmful lusts which drown men in destruction and perdition. For the love of money is a root of all kinds of evil, for which some have strayed from the faith in their greediness, and pierced themselves through with many sorrows.*

*1 Timothy 6: 9-10*

What do you desire from the Lord? Do you desire to be rich and famous? If to be rich is your motivation, it will never work. Honestly in my opinion, the goal of becoming rich shows lack of imagination and selfishness. It shows a desire to please oneself, and total disregard for others. God's gifts are for the benefit of the kingdom. His desire is for us to draw others unto him. The desire to serve must be greater than the desire for money.

Check your motives. Look beyond your current situations. Yes money is needed to survive in this world. However God promised to be our provider. Place your financial concerns at His feet and let Him do what He said He would do. The bible says your gift will make room for you. In other words, work the gift that God has given you, pursue His purpose and He will ensure you have everything and everyone you need to accomplish it.

The love of money causes people to stray from God. Why? Because they are consumed with making more money. The more money some have, the more they assume they do not need God. Without God we are nothing, we cease to exist. Examine yourself. How do you define success? Will you finally feel successful and accomplished once you have a certain amount of money? Money can come and go but the anointing and favor of God, no man can take away.

**PRAYER**: *Dear God show me the motives behind the desires of my heart. If I am motivated by anything that is not of you or is not beneficial to the kingdom, help me to remove them. Show me how to look beyond my present circumstances and seek how to use what you have given me to benefit the kingdom. In Jesus' name, Amen.*

## Reflection and Reaction

How do you define success?

What does it look like?

What do you desire in this life of the Lord?

# 15

# How "Big" is your Strength

*If you faint in the day of adversity, your strength is small.*

*Proverbs 24:10*

I love the book of Proverbs, reading it is like sitting down and talking with your grandmother. Proverbs provide wisdom for daily Christian living. This verse reminds me of two things:

1. Adversity is coming. Even when you are in God's will and He is ordering your steps, adversity is still coming. Adversity is not punishment. It comes to show us what we are capable of and to show how good God is for seeing us through. Adversity comes also to build character and produce patience.

2. If you faint, it is your own fault. The scripture says "your" strength is small. God has provided all we need to be victorious. Failure is a result of relying on our own strength. We are soldiers in the army of the Lord. God don't need no weak Christians. This walk, your purpose, requires strength. Not just any strength, but "Big" strength that comes in and from God.

Adversity is inevitable. If you feel yourself getting light-headed, ask yourself are you relying on your own strength or God's strength. Turn to the word and allow Him to rest, rule, and abide in your life.

**PRAYER:** *Lord help me to remember to turn to you first in times of trouble. For where I am weak, you are strong. In Jesus' name, Amen.*

## Reflection and Reaction

In what area(s) have you allowed your strength to weaken? Acknowledge it and ask God to give you His strength. For the word says He is made strong in our weakness.

# 16

# Established Steps

*In their hearts humans plan their course, but the Lord establishes their steps.*

*Proverbs 16:9 (NIV)*

When I first read this verse the first thing that came to mind is "the steps of a righteous man are ordered by the Lord." But there is a difference between order and establish.

- Order means a sequence or arrangement of successive things or the prescribed form or customary procedure.

- Establish means to place or settle in a secure position or condition. To make firm or secure. To cause to be recognized or accepted. To introduce and put into force. To prove validity or truth of.

When the Lord orders your steps, He provides you with a systematic order to accomplish your goals. However when your steps are established they are secured, validated, and recognized and accepted by others. When one is established he/she is promoted to a level of authority with God. Therefore establishment is a new level in God's plan for your life.

When God calls you, He provides the order and establishes the call. Therefore confirmation or validation from others is not necessary. God's word and His promises will accomplish its task in the Earth. God is very strategic and His plan requires patience and trust. Know that you are in His will, follow His plan, and watch Him work.

**PRAYER***: Dear Lord thank you for ordering and establishing my steps. Help me to relinquish my plans and rely on you for guidance in fulfilling your purpose. In Jesus' name, Amen.*

**Reflection and Reaction**

Have you already made plans and are frustrated that it didn't happen accordingly?

Submit your plans to God and be open for rearrangement.

# 17

# Kingdom Mindset

*Set your mind on things above, not on things on the earth. For you died, and your life is hidden with Christ in God.*

*Colossians 3: 2-3*

Make up your mind today. Be determined to focus on the promises of God. Make up your mind that God is in control. Make up your mind that you will trust Him no matter what. Stop speaking against his word by complaining about your problems. God is a positive God, negative thoughts go against His character.

Make up your mind that you will give God full control and complete access to your life. Take the limits off. Remove the restraints. There is nothing God can't handle. Give it to Him and keep it moving. Stop reviving the dead by focusing on what you can't control. Since you can't change your situation, change your mind.

You have work to do. Stop wasting time. Only God can reveal that which is hidden and He will not do so until the appointed time. Negativity keeps us in the wilderness. Grumbling and complaining along the journey will cause you to keep going around the same mountain. Positivity on the other hand, will make life a lot easier and the journey shorter.

Make up your mind that you will expect great things from God: Promotion, Increase, Favor, and Divine Connections. Change your mindset and watch God change your atmosphere.

**PRAYER:** *Lord help me to remember that you are in control and nothing can happen without your consent. Help me to change my attitude and set my mind on things above. In Jesus' name, Amen.*

**Reflection and Reaction**

What are you expecting from God?

Make up your mind that His word is true and expect it to come to pass.

# 18

# Be Opened

*Then looking up to heaven, He sighed and said to him, "Ephphatha," that is "Be Opened." Immediately his ears were opened and the impediment of his tongue was loosed, and he spoke plainly.*

*Mark 7: 34-35*

Ever wonder why people who are deaf, also have a speech impediment? I believe it is because what you speak is directly connected to what you hear and understand. If all you hear is negativity, from others, television, internet, etc.; then negativity will also come out of your mouth. But if you surround yourself with positivity, then your attitude, words, and actions will also be positive.

Do you hear the voice of the Lord? Do you understand what He is saying? In the quietness of day, God speaks, when you hear his voice then shall you speak. To hear God you must quiet your surroundings. God has not stopped talking, however we have stopped listening. There is too much noise. Noise causes confusion and frustration.

God wants to be alone with you, come unto Him, He is waiting. Remember you are God's mouthpiece in the Earth. If you don't take time to hear Him, you will not know what to speak.

**PRAYER***: Dear Lord help me to set aside quiet time specifically for you. Help me to listen to your voice and only speak when there is a clear understanding. In Jesus' name, Amen.*

**<u>Reflection and Reaction</u>**

Do you have a hard time hearing from the Lord?

How can you add time with the Lord to your daily routine? Get up early, stay up a few minutes late, on your lunch break, etc.

Make time for God and He will make time for you.

# 19

# In Jesus' Name

*And whatever you do in word or deed, do all in the name of the Lord Jesus, giving thanks to God the Father through Him.*

*Colossians 3: 17*

Remember that it's all for the Kingdom and the glory of God. When times get hard and they will get hard, remember it's for Jesus. When it seems like you are going backwards instead of forward, remember God has a plan. When others don't understand your purpose, and you feel like you are all alone, remember God is with you.

To whom much is given, much is required. God chose you because you can handle it and you are well equipped for the job. It is very important that you remain in the word and heed the voice of the Lord. God only tells us the end. Such as you will have your own company, or you will be this or have that. He does not disclose all we will have to go through to get to the promise, because most of us will give up.

Remember the road to greatness is one of joy along with heartache. But in the end, God gets the glory. And what God has ordained, no man can change. If and when God leads you there, He will keep you there. Give thanks to God for the good and the struggles; in the end we have the victory.

**PRAYER:** *Lord thank you for the plan that you have laid out for my life. In the hard times, help me to remember that it is all in your name and that you are always with me. In Jesus' name, Amen.*

**<u>Reflection and Reaction</u>**

What can you do to remind yourself that it is all for Jesus and the kingdom? Who are you serving or can you serve?

Reflect daily on those you are serving and watch your attitude and mind change.

# 20

# Walk in the Spirit

*And those who are Christ's have crucified the flesh with its passions and desires. If we live in the Spirit, let us also walk in the Spirit. Let us not become conceited, provoking one another, envying one another.*

*Galatians 5: 24-26*

What does it mean to walk in the Spirit? Does it mean you should ignore the cares of the world or your present circumstances? Does it mean that you have a distorted view of reality? Does it mean that you refuse to live in the moment?

To walk in the Spirit, does not mean you ignore what is going on in your life or your current issues, rather it means you give God your problems and allow Him free reign to handle them. It means you pray about everything and worry about nothing. It means you don't allow your issues to consume you.

To walk in the Spirit, does not mean you have a distorted view of reality, rather it means that your present does not define who you are. You don't become frustrated because you don't understand how God is working things out. You trust that He is always working on your behalf. Even when you don't understand, you have faith that He will fulfill His promise. You have patience and know that in His perfect timing all things will be clear.

To walk in the Spirit, does not mean you refuse to live in the moment, but rather you praise Him for every moment. You recognize God's awesome power in your life. You see the work of His hands in your past, present and future. You understand that the journey to the promise is just as important as arriving at the Promised Land.

**PRAYER:** *Dear Heavenly Father, thank you for your Holy Spirit leading and guiding me into all truths. Help me to continue to walk in the Spirit and place all my cares, frustrations, and self-doubt at your feet. In Jesus' name, Amen.*

**Reflection and Reaction**

How do you define walking in the Spirit?

What changes can you make to begin to eliminate the reoccurring stumbling blocks in your walk?

# 21

# Who is Holding Your Ladder?

*Brethren, if a man is overtaken in any trespass, you who are spiritual restore such a one in a spirit of gentleness, considering yourself lest you also be tempted. Bear one another's burdens, and so fulfill the law of Christ. For if anyone thinks himself to be something, when he is nothing, he deceives himself.*

*Galatians 6: 1-3*

We have all heard of the cliché, "Be careful of the toes you step on or cross on the way up the ladder as they may be attached to the faces you may see coming down." (That's the clean version) But this statement implies that one may fail. Failure is not my concern today.

My concern is, who will be there for you when going up the ladder gets hard? When you are experiencing fear? When you need encouragement or reassurance? Yes sometimes you have to encourage yourself. But sometimes life hits you so hard, that it leaves you speechless.

You will need someone in your corner. A prayer warrior who will petition the throne on your behalf. Someone who knows your purpose. Someone who is supportive of your goals and dreams. Someone who will dare you and challenge you to keep going. Someone who will give you a shoulder to lean on and not gossip about your weaknesses behind your back.

If you assume that no one understands you. No one is like you. Everyone is jealous. Everyone is a hater. You will find that when you reach the top of the ladder, no one is at the bottom holding your position. Ensuring you don't fall. Cheering you on as you go up.

There will be people in your life who will be negative and non-supportive. Pray for them, that God opens their spiritual eyes. Don't think you are too good or better than them. But there are others who have genuine love and support for you and of the God in you. Treat them with gentleness. Take their constructive criticism to heart. Don't despise their advice and teaching. Cherish those friendships and give them their flowers while you can. There will be places on the road to success in which you will have to go alone but don't choose to travel alone if you don't have to.

**PRAYER:** *Dear Heavenly Father, thank you for the valuable friendships you have placed in my life. Help me to nurture and cherish those individuals as I journey towards my purpose. In Jesus' name, Amen.*

**Reflection and Reaction**

Are their some relationships you need to mend?

Have you burned bridges that you now realize you need to get to the other side?

Ask God for forgiveness and then for strength to apologize to those you took for granted.

# 22

# Settling for Mediocrity

*The thief does not come except to steal, and to kill, and to destroy. I have come that they may have life, and that they may have it more abundantly.*

*John 10: 10*

When did "average" become the standard? We have developed an "everybody's doing it, so it must be right mentality." Who dares to stand out among the crowd? Successful people do, that's who.

Life happens to us all. Sometimes those circumstances are used by the devil to keep you from being or becoming who God designed you to be. But only if you let it. The enemy's job is to steal your joy, kill your dreams, and destroy your future. But Jesus came to give you an alternative.

You no longer have to settle for living in poverty, living pay check to pay check, or a lifestyle in survival mode: if I can just make it to… (Fill in the blank). Mediocrity is a choice. You don't have to settle for the hand that life dealt or that was dealt to your ancestors. You can decide to break the curse. You can decide to get off the train, get in a car and take control.

The number one step to moving out of mediocrity; out of survival mode into thriving mode is to analyze who you associate with. If your circle of friends consists of the nothing clan: ain't got nothing and don't want nothing; then you need to find a new circle. We tend to hang on to folks because we grew up with them, went to school with them, or they had your back when such and such happened. But the truth is you have out grown them. Your values and dreams have changed. You want better for yourself. It's ok, God told us to love all people, not spend all our time with all people.

Your circle should consist of people who bring out the best in you. They should challenge you to do better and be a better person. They should push you or pull you, kicking and screaming if need be, into your purpose. Wise people hang around wise people. Successful people hang around other successful people. Greatness begets greatness. You glean from those closest to you. What are you learning?

**PRAYER:** *Dear Heavenly Father, help me to examine those around me. Give me wisdom to discern those who are good for me and sent by you. Give me strength to limit my time or to walk away from those who are not of you or are not good for me. Help me to walk in the abundant life that you freely gave to me. In Jesus' name, Amen.*

## Reflection and Reaction

In what ways have you accepted mediocrity?

Examine your circle, as well as your lifestyle.

Who or what is holding you back?

# 23

# My Sheep Know My Voice

*But he who enters by the door is the shepherd of the sheep. To him the doorkeeper opens, and the sheep hear his voice, and he calls his own sheep by name and leads them out. And when he brings out his own sheep, he goes before them; and the sheep follow him, for they know his voice. Yet they will by no means follow a stranger, but will flee from him, for they do not know the voice of strangers.*

*John 10: 2 – 5*

Do you know the voice of the Lord? Yes you say? Then why are you questioning God? Why are you looking for confirmation from the Prophet, Pastor, Mother, Evangelist, Minister, etc.? The same God that is in them is the same God that is in you. God is no respecter of persons, what He does for one, He can and will do for all. Don't allow your fear or need for recognition to allow you to miss the favor of God in your life.

Whose voice are you listening to? Jesus, you say? Then why are you allowing hypocrites, non-believers, haters, etc. to talk you out of what God has said. Why are you conferring with the enemy? God is not a liar and His word will not return to Him void. God's way is the only way. Don't allow the disappointment and mistakes of others to chart your destiny. You are not like them...You are following the voice of the Lord.

All of God's gifts come with an appointed time. Don't allow fear and doubt to cause you to miss your season of favor. As you go, you will learn to quiet the voice of the enemy. As you go, fear and doubt will disappear. Allow God to accomplish His promise in you. Do not be afraid.

**PRAYER:** *Dear Heavenly Father, thank you for your Holy Spirit leading and guiding me. Help me to stay focused on your plans for my life. I bind distraction, fear, doubt, and the voice of the enemy that comes to throw me off course. In Jesus' name, Amen.*

## Reflection and Reaction

Many times distractions, people, things or activities, can cause us not to hear God's voice.

Analyze your daily activities. What are you listening to? What are you watching on television? Are the activities you choose for entertainment edifying to your body and mind? Do they invoke feelings of positivity or negativity?

How can you replace these activities with things that are pleasing to God and build your relationship with Him?

# 24

# God is With You

*Have I not commanded you? Be strong and of good courage; do not be afraid, nor be dismayed, for the Lord your God is with you wherever you go.*

*Joshua 1: 9*

Has the Lord already given you instructions? Has He already revealed your purpose? Do you know how He wants you to use your gift in the Earth to benefit the kingdom? The hardest task in walking in your calling is believing you can do it. God did not make a mistake. You are the one He chose, you are more than capable.

We talk ourselves out of doing before we even start. Some make a great start, but run out of steam in the middle. Things get hard. Everyone is not on your side. Negativity surrounds you. It seems like you are taking two steps backward rather than a step forward. But God will not be mocked. Jesus was not received in His own city. God will give you your hater's reward. His word promises He will prepare a table before you in the presence of your enemies.

God exalts and God promotes, so don't look for recognition from man. There is no need to be afraid or to second guess God or your purpose. God is ordering your steps, He is with you always. Unfortunately pain is also a part of the plan. He is building character. Just don't give up! Your appointed time is now. You are the only one who can halt God's hand, if you give up. You shall reap if you faint not.

**PRAYER:** *Dear God thank you for sending your angels before me to prepare the way. Help me to have confidence in you and not my own abilities. Your will be done in my life. In Jesus' name, Amen.*

**<u>Reflection and Reaction</u>**

In what ways have you forgotten God is with you?

How can you be reminded?

# 25

# Something Told Me

*Your ears shall hear a word behind you, saying, "This is the way, walk in it," whenever you turn to the right hand or whenever you turn to the left.*

*Isaiah 30:21*

Many people like to say "something told me to do this and that" or "woman's intuition" led them to a grave discovery. But we are Christians, the Holy Spirit lives in us, leading us to all truths. That small still voice has a name. He is never wrong.

Why is it that we are quick to listen to "something told me" or "my woman's intuition said go" but when the Lord gives us explicit instructions we are hesitant and allow fear to rise? God's instructions usually defy logic. It doesn't make sense to our natural minds. We question him and then try to justify it by saying because it appeared to make no sense, it couldn't have been God.

God is omnipresent. He sees all things, hears all things, and knows all things. He will not allow you to fail. Failure only comes if you do it your own way. His voice is soft, His instructions are clear, do not hesitate, and do not fear. Do not allow your own questioning to allow you to miss the move of God in your life. Where you go requires complete trust in God, belief in His power, and faith in His abilities.

**PRAYER:** *Dear God thank you for your presence in my life. Help me to trust you and to surrender to your will. In Jesus' name, Amen.*

## Reflection and Reaction

What does the voice of the Lord sound like? How do you know that it is Him?

Trust Him and don't allow the enemy to make you doubt what you hear.

# 26

# Your First Love

*Nevertheless, I have this against you, that you have left your first love.*

*Revelation 2:4*

How soon we forget. Remember how the Lord waited patiently for you? Remember that night when you cried yourself to sleep and He wrapped His arms of peace around you? Remember how He shielded you when the enemy tried to take you out? Remember how He comforted you when that love one passed away or when that man broke your heart?

The word says "With lovingkindness has He drawn you". Yet how soon you forget that He is the same God. The same God who comforted you, protected you, cared for you, and patiently waited for you then is the same God who can do it for you now. Now that the heat has intensified or the problem seems bigger, you decide not even God can help you. If He was faithful then, He is faithful now. If He was able then, He is able now.

Lay your problems, concerns, and worries at His feet and allow Him to show you who He is. You are not alone. You are already victorious. The more you allow your problems to weigh you down the less energy you will have to pursue your purpose. He is concerned about all that concerns you, cast your cares upon Him.

**PRAYER:** *Dear Heavenly Father, thank you for caring for me. You see all and know all. Look upon my problems, my finances, my worries, and my concerns and grant me your peace that surpasses all understanding. Help me to remember that all things are working for my good and that I have the victory as long as I keep my eyes stayed on you. In Jesus' name, Amen.*

## Reflection and Reaction

It's time to return to your first love.

Reflect on the day you got saved. What is your salvation story? Remember He is the same God.

# 27

# Perfection in God

---

*The Lord will perfect that which concerns me; Your mercy, O Lord, endures forever; do not forsake the works of Your hands.*

*Psalms 138:8*

He will make you perfect. How? Why? Through His grace, because His mercy endures forever. You are His name sake, He will not leave you helpless. But "nobody is perfect" says the world. True, but in Him, because of Him, by His grace, because of His love, you are being perfected every day.

The more time you spend with God, learning of his character and His thoughts for you and towards you, the more you want to please Him. Because He first loved you. He came for you. He was persecuted for you. He died for you. He rose for you. And for Him, all He asks, is that you live for Him, obey His commandments, and tell others of His love.

God's love teaches us to love others. It is in this love and because of His love that we are perfected. Anything that you lack, He will perfect. Where you are weak, He will perfect. Only trust Him. Believe in His promises and have faith that He can do the impossible.

**PRAYER:** *Dear God thank you for your mercy and your grace. Thank you for perfecting everything that concerns me. Help me to walk in your grace. In Jesus' name, Amen.*

**Reflection and Reaction**

How are you being perfected in Him?

Think back to how you were 3, 5, even 10 years ago?

Age does not change people, God does! Praise God! Ain't He good!

___

___

# 28

# Shout With a Great Shout

*It shall come to pass, when they make a long blast with the ram's horn, and when you hear the sound of the trumpet, that all the people shall shout with a great shout; then the wall of the city will fall down flat. And the people shall go up every man straight before him.*

*Joshua 6: 5*

Joshua must have thought it crazy that he could march around a city seven times, shout, and the walls would come tumbling down. But jump down to verse 20 and that's exactly what happened. Is that kind of confidence in God possible today? I love this passage for two reasons:

1. What seems impossible to us is possible with God. Does the task before you seem too difficult? Do you feel as though you lack the skills or the ability? Good, that way when it happens you can't take the credit. If you could do it on your own or through others, there would be no need for God. Sometimes we just need to sit back and watch God work.

2. A good shout, can bring down walls. Why have you allowed the enemy to silence you? At your word, walls fall, mountains are moved, storms cease, and demons flee. If nothing is happening in your life, it may be because you ain't saying nothing. Open your mouth and stop letting the enemy walk all over you. Your silence means you are in agreement.

God is not slack concerning His promises. That company, that husband, that dream is yours. Just trust and believe nothing is impossible. Get your war cry on. When the enemy tells you, you are inadequate, shout JESUS! When the enemy tells you, you are not good enough, shout JESUS! When the enemy tells you, you are too old to make your dreams come true, shout JESUS! All power is in His name.

**PRAYER:** *Heavenly Father, I thank you that I already have the victory. Help me to heed to your voice and trust in your word. Help me to remember that it is because of your grace and favor, I am worthy. Because* *you chose me, I am capable. And because of your blood, I am victorious. In Jesus' name, Amen.*

## Reflection and Reaction

Has the enemy silenced you?

Open your mouth and shout your way to victory!

# 29

# Let Your Light Shine

*In Him was life, and the life was the light of men. And the light shines in the darkness, and the darkness did not comprehend.*

*John 1: 4-5*

God is the light in the darkness of your past, but because you do not understand you do not allow Him to shine. You were made to tell of His goodness. Once you realize who you are, you will be ready for His use. You are a child of God born of God. You are in His bosom, He has declared you righteous.

Many believe God does not enter the scene or become active in our lives until the day we accept salvation. But God is in us and has been with us from birth, actually before he formed us in the womb. And we try to comprehend or figure out how things in our life, bad things can happen. We blame ourselves and harbor a lot of anger, regret and un-forgiveness. Truth is the fact that we are here today and still able to tell the story is a testament to the love God has for us, because He could have allowed the enemy to kill us. The very thing we are condemning ourselves for, or allowing to hold us down because of fear is the very thing that God will use to reach others. True forgiveness is letting go of the thoughts that the past could have been different. We can't change it. God was merely preparing us for our time, our platform.

If you allow the past to control your present, your future will never exist.

If you don't do what you are supposed to do today, tomorrow you will be playing catch up.

If you spend today worried about yesterday, you won't know when tomorrow comes.

**PRAYER:** *Dear Heavenly Father. I thank you for the victories of my past. Help me to see who you are and what you did rather than the devastation of what happened. I submit myself to your will and relinquish control to you. Your will be done in my life, In Jesus' name, Amen.*

**Reflection and Reaction**

What area in your past has caused your light to dim?

Ask God to reveal His protection that you may get a deeper appreciation of the survival rather than the victimization.

# 30

# Stand in the Silence

*Therefore take up the whole armor of God, that you may be able to withstand in the evil day, and having done all to stand.*

*Ephesians 6: 13*

There will come a time in the journey in which God will appear to be silent. This silence can be intentional to test your faith. Or the silence can be assumed, due to the onset of fear.

God never promised the journey would be without pain or discomfort. In fact the pain and discomfort are part of the plan. Don't revert to plan B and assume that because it is not going smoothly that you are going in the wrong direction. Trust that God knows what is best.

Sometimes the difficulty of the journey can intensify the voice of fear. You begin to question your abilities and even start to tell God how you are not fit for the task. If you could do it in your own abilities, there would be no need for God. Stop saying and focusing on what you can't do and do what you can. Sometimes when you start doing, you will realize you can do more than you thought.

If the instructions are not clear, stand in the silence.

If you can't hear God's voice, stand in the silence.

You must quiet your thoughts to hear God. The loudness of fear is drowning out His voice. Wait until you can hear clearly.

**PRAYER:** *Dear God, I thank you that you are ordering and establishing my steps. Help me to quiet the voice of fear and rely on your strength and abilities rather than focus on my weaknesses. In Jesus' name, Amen.*

## Reflection and Reaction

What fear has come upon you that prevents you from hearing God and heeding His instructions?

Write down the fear, then write down the scripture that provides a promise to cancel that fear.

# 31

# Mighty in Battle

*All these kings and their land Joshua took at one time, because the Lord God of Israel fought for Israel.*

*Joshua 10: 42*

Joshua faced five, yes five, Amorite kings. He did not cower down and tell God "that's too many to take on at one time" or "which one do you want me to fight first." He trusted God and went in for battle. As women we pride ourselves on being great at multi-tasking. We come in from work, put dinner on, help the kids with homework, iron school clothes for tomorrow, run bath water, and feed the children, all before 9:00pm. Where did the time go? When faced with many tasks, did we give up and say "it's too much to handle"?

When it comes to the things of God, on the other hand, we tend to question His timing, His order and our ability. God you sure you want me to do all that? Which one do you want me to do first? I can't possibly do all that at one time! God is trying to hand you the keys to the kingdom. He has given you the land, and you are settling for one key at a time, one acre at a time.

If we could only grasp the principle that Joshua discovered. God is on the frontline. He is fighting for us. He is the ultimate multi-tasker. The enemy, regardless of how large in number, is no match for the army of God. You already have the victory, God is only requiring your obedience.

**PRAYER**: *Dear God, thank you for fighting on my behalf. Help me to remember that the battle is already won. Open my spiritual ears, so that I may hear your voice clearly, and quicken to your command. In Jesus' name, Amen.*

## Reflection and Reaction

How many tasks are you juggling?

Which ones were given to you by God?

In your fear or lack of understanding, have you put your own desires before God?

How can you make more time for God and the things of God?

# 32

# Because of Your Unbelief

*Now He did not do many mighty works there because of their unbelief.*

*Matthew 13:58*

Many people like to say "what God has for me is for me." This is a true concept in theory. But there is one thing that can delay your blessings. Unbelief. The negativity of others cannot stop God's movement in your life. However your own negativity, doubt, skepticism, and lack of faith are a result of unbelief and will stop the mighty works of God in your life.

To not believe in God is to reject Him. To doubt what He has said is to reject Him. He cannot work in unbelief. When things get hard, remember the Word. It will almost always get worse before it gets better. There is no testimony without a test. Murmuring and complaining causes you to fail the test. Failure means repeat. Remember the children of Israel wandered in the desert forty years because of their lack of faith. That generation never saw the Promised Land.

Remember what God has spoken over you. Go through as a good soldier. Watch and pray! Meditate on the word. Wait on the Lord with joyful expectation and watch Him work on your behalf.

**PRAYER:** *Dear Heavenly Father. Help my unbelief. Help me to remember that you are not slack concerning the promises toward me. Help me to be thankful in all things. In Jesus' name, Amen.*

**<u>Reflection and Reaction</u>**

What has God promised you? Make a list and read them daily.

Whenever unbelief creeps in, bring out the list and begin to thank God for them in advance.

________________________________________________________

________________________________________________________

# 33

# What Are You Asking?

*And in that day you will ask Me nothing. Most assuredly, I say to you, whatever you ask the Father in My name He will give you. Until now you have asked nothing in My name. Ask, and you will receive, that your joy may be full.*

*John 16:23-24*

God is concerned with the heart of man. Your heart must be open to receive Him and follow His commands. But who told you, you had to be perfect to come to Jesus or to ask things of Him? Perfect speech, perfect intelligence, perfect obedience, perfect Christian? In Him you are perfect. He is not concerned with how you come, but that you come, and that your relationship with Him will bring about transformation. Jesus said come as you are, but you should not leave as you came.

What are you asking? People like to say that God is not listening or that He does not answer prayers. I ask what are you asking Him? If you ask God the right question He will always answer. Remember His blessings also come with an appointed time. So perhaps you are asking for something out of season. So if God is not giving what you ask. Ask Him what does He want you to have? God gives according to His will, not just because you want it.

Don't allow your lack of perfection or lustful desires to keep you from seeking God. Study the word. Meditate on it day and night. Open your mouth. Declare His word over your desires and circumstances. Ask what you desire and watch Him perform it. Be patient. Patience proves your love and trust in God's abilities.

**PRAYER:** *Dear God thank you for declaring me righteous through your shed blood on the cross. Help me to remember that it is not perfection that is required to come to you but belief that you are listening. Help me to line up my desires with your will for my life. In Jesus' name, Amen.*

## Reflection and Reaction

Examine your requests:

What are you asking God for? Are they in line with His purpose and plan for your life? Or are they full of materialistic wants based in covetousness?

# 34

# Remember Your Vows

*Then she made a vow and said, "O Lord of hosts, if You will indeed look on the affliction of Your maidservant and remember me, and not forget Your maidservant, but will give Your maidservant a male child, then I will give him to the Lord all the days of his life, and no razor shall come upon his head."*

*1 Samuel 1: 11*

*So it came to pass in the process of time that Hannah conceived and bore a son, and called his name Samuel, saying "Because I have asked for him from the Lord."*

*1 Samuel 1: 20*

What have you asked of the Lord? What promises have you made to ensure you get it? Lord if you bless me with a better job or more money, I will pay my tithes faithfully. Lord if you send me my husband, I will put You first in my marriage. Lord if you help me out of this mess, I will serve you. Lord if you do this, I will do that. But how soon do we forget. God remembers His promises toward us, and He also remembers the vows we made toward Him.

Ecclesiastes 5: 4-5 states "When you make a vow to God do not delay to pay it; for He has no pleasure in fools. Pay what you have vowed – Better not to vow than to vow and not pay." God is faithful, He expects us to be faithful as well. Be careful what you ask for. The sacrifices required to keep it will be great. Whether it is a child, like Hannah, a husband, a job, company, or whatever you desire from the Lord. Keep your vow. Offer it as a sacrifice unto the Lord and allow His glory to be revealed.

**PRAYER:** *Dear heavenly Father, thank you for your faithfulness towards me. Help me to be patient and wait, with expectation, for you to grant me the desires of my heart. Help me to remember the vows I have made toward you, regarding those desires, that I may keep them. In Jesus' name, Amen.*

**Reflection and Reaction**

Did you make a promise to God in exchange for a desire or need?

Be sure to keep your end of the bargain. Your word is your bond.

Can God trust you?

# 35

# Managing Your Time Wisely

*See then that you walk circumspectly, not as fools but as wise, redeeming the time, because the days are evil. Therefore do not be unwise, but understand what the will of the Lord is.*

*Ephesians 5: 15-17:*

Have you ever come to the end of the day and wondered where did the time go? Spent hours on Facebook, playing video games, watching TV, or day dreaming, when you could have been doing countless other things? Technology has consumed our time. But God is calling us to be productive. To redeem the time means to spend our time wisely.

Be mindful of wasteful activities. Steve Harvey, once said "if it ain't making you no money, don't spend time doing it." Yes there is a need for relaxation activities. Even God rested on the 7th day. But we should set goals. What do you want to accomplish each day, this week, this month, this year, in five years? If we do not plan to succeed, we plan to fail. Put time limits on your goals, and stick with them.

Be mindful of who you spend your time with. Some people are in your life for a season, don't spend too much time with people whose season is over. Just because they are your BFF, or you have known them all your life does not mean they belong in this season of your life. If you hang around wise people, you will become wise. If you hang around people who are bitter, angry, or living in mediocrity, so shall you be also. Don't be afraid to cut off people who no longer add to your current life, who don't know who you are, don't value who you have become, or don't push you into your destiny.

Wasted time can't be retrieved, but with each new day God has given you the opportunity to start again. End each day with no regrets. Fill each day pursuing the purpose God gave you at creation.

**PRAYER***: Dear Heavenly Father. This is the day you have made, I will rejoice and be glad in it. Help me to stay focused today on your will* *for my life. Quickly remind me of any time that I am not spending wisely. In Jesus' name, Amen.*

## Reflection and Reaction

What activities fill most of your day?

Keep track of your time for a week. What people or activities do you spend most of your time with or doing? (Talking on the phone, hanging out, social media, games, etc.)

Are the activities or people helping you reach your goals?

# 36

# Who is God?

*He said to them "But who do you say that I am?"*

*Matthew 16:15*

Who is God to you? Do you believe that He is the "Great I Am" in you? The greater you want to become is available to you now through the one who lives in you. Just because you don't have what you want right now does not mean you are not capable of achieving it or worthy of receiving it.

Who you believe God to be is tied to your trust in Him. You lack trust because your thought process is one sided. You only think in terms of what you don't have. Be mindful of what you do have and have already accomplished. If you must, literally take inventory of your accomplishments. Type them up in a word document in large print. Print it out, make copies and post them in as many places as need be to remind you of what God has done.

Sometimes we take on more than we should because we will not allow God to be God in our lives or over our situations and circumstances. God is a gentleman, if you want Him to open your door, you must step aside, wait, and allow Him to do so. You are not alone. It is not you against the world. God can make the world your footstool all He requires is trust and faith in Him.

**PRAYER**: *Heavenly Father, thank you for allowing your strength and power to rest, rule and abide in me. Help me to be mindful of what you have already done in my life and what you are going to do now and in the future. In Jesus' name, Amen.*

(Today's devotional is an excerpt from my book entitled *Stop Asking Me Why Am I Single*)

## Reflection and Reaction

Who is God to you?

Is He a genie or magician making all your wishes come true? Is He on a pedestal, too high for you to touch? Is He the first choice or last resort in a difficult situation? Is He like fine china you bring out to impress others?

Our ability to trust God is coincides with our view of His power and understanding of His character.

# 37

# Wisdom Revealed in His Word

*But as it is written: "Eye has not seen, nor ear heard, nor have entered into the heart of man the things which God has prepared for those who love Him." But God has revealed them to us through His Spirit. For the Spirit searches all things, yes, the deep things of God. For what man knows the things of a man except the spirit of the man which is in him? Even so no one knows the things of God except the Spirit of God. Now we have received, not the spirit of the world, but the Spirit who is from God, that we might know the things that have been freely given to us by God.*

*1 Corinthians 2: 9-12*

The wisdom of God resides in His word. The preacher can't give it to you. The mothers or ministers can't pray it into you. No matter how good your pastor preaches and teaches, no matter how many praying mothers have laid hands on you; there comes a time when you must know the Lord for yourself. To receive God's wisdom, to know His plans for your life, you must actively pursue Him. Regular time reading and studying the word cannot be ignored.

Once God's plan is revealed, there is no need to verify with others. Faith is required for progression. You must be willing to put yourself in a position to drown. There ain't no plan B. It's God's way or no way. You must learn to hear the voice of the Lord and quickly obey. Don't give the enemy time to throw in doubt and fear. It won't be easy, because there will be times when it will appear you are going backwards, but trust that God knows what is best.

**PRAYER:** *Father God thank you for your Holy Spirit living in me, revealing all truths and guiding me according to the plan you have for my life. Help me to remove all barriers that hinder me from hearing your voice. Help me to remember that you are my shepherd, and no matter how tough it may seem, I shall not want. In Jesus' name, Amen.*

## Reflection and Reaction

Reflect on the person you were when you first got saved and the person you are today?

Have you grown in wisdom or do you continue to make the same mistakes and same poor choices?

How does your relationship with God factor into your current lifestyle?

# 38

# God is Love

*To know the love of Christ which passes knowledge; that you may be filled with all fullness of God*

*Ephesians 3: 19*

God is love. This statement tends to be the explanation for or against just about everything. God is love, is used to explain why sin is ok, because God loves everyone. God is love is used in anger, because how could a loving God allow bad things to happen to good people. But what does this statement really mean. John 3:16 tells us how God so loved the world that He gave His only begotten son. So God's love is followed by sacrificial acts.

So if God is love and we are to show His love to others, what sacrifices are we making? Ephesians 3:19 tells us that the love of Christ passes knowledge. So then how do we know the love of Christ? How do we know what His expression of love will or will not do? We learn of God's love through His word and by the guidance of the Holy Spirit.

> *What I have in my spirit is a gift from God. That's where it will stay if I don't learn to be led by the Holy Spirit. What I have in my spirit is what Christ has done for me. How I live is what I do for Christ. What I have in my spirit is not my character; it is my position in Christ.*
> *-Joyce Myers*

Our actions, emotions, feelings, etc. are not of God because of selfish ambition or pleasure seeking. This is the sinful nature that we all were born into. In order to become Christ-like, to act like Him, to think like Him, to allow His will to override our will, we must submit to the teachings and guidance of the Holy Spirit…..that we may be filled with all fullness of God.

**PRAYER:** *Heavenly Father thank you for the love you have given me. Help me to show your love daily in how I live my life. Help me to be an example of your love to all that I encounter. Let your glory be revealed in me, that others will see the depth and trueness of your love. In Jesus' name, Amen.*

**Reflection and Reaction**

What does love look like to you? What does it feel like?

How does your perception of love influence your actions toward others? Toward God?

# 39

# Consider the Ant

*Go to the ant, you sluggard! Consider her ways and be wise, which, having no captain, overseer or ruler, provides her supplies in the summer, and gathers her food in the harvest. How long will you slumber, O sluggard? When will you rise from your sleep? A little sleep, a little slumber, a little folding of the hands to sleep— so shall your poverty come on you like a prowler, and your need like an armed man.*

*Proverbs 6: 6-11*

The Ant! The smallest creature, God created. The pest we try to rid our homes and yards from. The one who we feel spoil our summer fun at the park. The Ant! That which we deem as a pest, God says is wise. I never really thought about the ant until one Sunday morning, when my pastor taught us this word.

Every ant in the colony has its own responsibility. The colony consists of the queen, the winged male, the worker and the soldier. The worker and the soldier are also females. The queen's job is to produce eggs to multiply the colony. The worker feeds the queen and the soldier protects the worker. But what about the winged male? The winged male is born from an unknown substance. The male's only job is to impregnate the queen, and then he dies! Did you know, that if an ant goes out and gets a fungus or infection, the other ants will lick the fungus to take away some of the illness so that the sick ant will not perish. The colony is dependent on everyone surviving.

"Consider her ways and be wise" says the Lord. If even the smallest creature, with everything else under God's creation considered its enemy, can be about His father's business. We certainly have no excuse. The ant does not stop, everyday it awakens to fulfill its purpose. Sluggard! What has distracted you? Your purpose, objective, or goals, should shape everything you do, and thus compound your chances for success. There is no failure in God.

Ever wondered why things don't seem to be going right? Why your bank account is empty before the end of the day on payday? Why no matter what you do, your efforts are unproductive? Are you doing what God called you to do or are you pursuing your own plans. The word says "A man's heart plans his way, but the LORD directs his steps." (Proverbs 16:9). What goals have you set? Were these goals from God?

Examine your ways. Consider the ant. Submit yourself and your plans to God's will and plan for your life. Minimize your engagement in activities that draw you from God and His plan. Recommit to do His purpose and His will and watch His glory manifest in your life.

**PRAYER:** *Dear Heavenly Father, thank you for the plans you have outlined for my life. Today I recommit to do your will and your purpose. I recognize I cannot obtain success without your guidance. Thank you for your Holy Spirit. I ask that you set me in alignment this week with your truth, your way, your purpose and your will. I recognize that it is no longer about doing but about being whom you created me to be. I bind confusion right now in the name of Jesus and ask for clarity of your specific purpose for my life. In Jesus' name, Amen.*

## Reflection and Reaction

Laziness produces poverty.

How bad do you want it?

Success is available if you are willing to work hard.

What actions can you begin today to make your goals, God's plan a reality?

___________________________________________

___________________________________________

___________________________________________

___________________________________________

___________________________________________

___________________________________________

___________________________________________

# 40

# What Kind of Tree Are You?

*"The Spirit of the Lord GOD is upon Me, Because the LORD has anointed Me to preach good tidings to the poor; He has sent Me to heal the brokenhearted, to proclaim liberty to the captives, and the opening of the prison to those who are bound; to proclaim the acceptable year of the LORD, and the day of vengeance of our God; to comfort all who mourn, to console those who mourn in Zion, to give them beauty for ashes, the oil of joy for mourning, the garment of praise for the spirit of heaviness; that they may be called trees of righteousness, the planting of the LORD, that He may be glorified."*

*Isaiah 61: 1-3*

Sometimes things just don't feel good. Even as Christians we have days when things don't go right, something or somebody rubs us the wrong way, or we just woke up on the wrong side of the bed. We don't feel like smiling. We don't feel like praying. We don't feel like thanking God. But the word tells us the just shall live by faith. It's not about our feelings.

The day of vengeance is upon us. Jesus has promised beauty for ashes, oil of joy for morning, and the garment of praise for the spirit of heaviness. No matter how the day began, unveiled, or ended…this is the day that the Lord made and we must choose to rejoice and be glad in it. God expects us to show love anyway, to smile any way, to praise Him anyway. We are trees of righteousness, planted by Him that He may be glorified.

What kind of tree are you? When the winds blow and storms come, are you easily uprooted and topple over? What kind of tree are you? Are you waiting on people to build you up or confirm God's call on your life? Bloom where you are planted. If God planted you there, stay there and take up root. Make up your mind that you are going to stand on the word. Your Christian walk should not be up and down. You either believe the word or you don't. You are either in this thing, on God's team or you ain't.

A tree of righteousness brings forth the glory of God. It is easily identified with the presence and power of God. It always has the mindset of preparing for His return. It is his choice, desire, and intention to please the Lord. A tree of righteousness is lined up with God. We are in Christ, and therefore look at life through His lens. All feelings are placed to the side and we've just got to do it!

**PRAYER:** *Heavenly Father, I just thank you on today. I thank you for beauty for ashes. I thank you for oil of joy for mourning. I thank you for the garment of praise when I feel heavy. Help my unbelief. Increase my faith. Help me to keep my mind focused on things above and not on what it looks like in front of me. Create in me a clean heart that I may desire your will and your righteousness. In Jesus' name, Amen.*

## Reflection and Reaction

In order to know what tree you are, you must examine your roots.

Are your roots weak with bitterness, anger, etc. that will cause you to topple over at the break of a storm?

Are your roots strengthened in love, kindness, the fruits of the spirt that you are able to bloom where you are planted?

_______________________________________________

_______________________________________________

_______________________________________________

_______________________________________________

_______________________________________________

_______________________________________________

_______________________________________________

_______________________________________________

_______________________________________________

_______________________________________________

_______________________________________________

_______________________________________________

_______________________________________________

# 41

# Limited Funding With Unlimited Dreams

*...that the God of our Lord Jesus Christ, the Father of glory, may give to you the spirit of wisdom and revelation in the knowledge of Him, the eyes of your understanding being enlightened, that you may know what is the hope of His calling, what are the riches of the glory of His inheritance in the Saints, and what is the exceeding greatness of His power toward us who believe, according to the working of His mighty power.*

*Ephesians 1: 17-19*

Who is God to you? Is He someone you call upon when all others have failed? Is He convenience among exasperated possibilities? Is He the last resort? Is He All Mighty, All Powerful, All Seeing, and All Knowing? Do you even know who He is? The reading of scripture gives us insight into God's character and unconditional love for His people. But it is the knowing of Him for yourself, the personal testimony, which provides the knowledge of Him. It is the "...But God" moments that produce the unshakable faith that is Christian, that is characteristic of His disciples.

Do we believe God is all and has all? Then why are we so easily distracted. The pursuit of money, material, and power has blinded our sight into the hope of His calling. Whatever He has called us to do, we are to have hope that He will complete that work in us. Yet we allow money to either hinder us or fuel us. Hinder us in that, lack of money will cause us to procrastinate. "I don't have any money, surely God is not talking about doing this and that now, He knows I can't afford it. Surely He does not want me to go into debt," we say. Money can fuel us, in that the pursuit of wealth can change our motives. What started as the will of the Lord to bless and benefit the kingdom can become selfish ambition in pursuit of fame and fortune.

God has all riches. Money should not make you doubt Him or question His voice. Don't allow a temporary cash flow to make you miss the move of God. All blessings come with an appointed season, who knows when or if it may come again. Don't get caught up in how or when you will make money, the bible states your gift will make room for you. God promised to supply all your needs. Examine yourself daily. Study the word daily. Listen to the prompting of the Holy Spirit. Stay humble and if you find yourself drifting, pray, fast, meditate, and then pray some more. All we need to do is believe, God will handle the rest.

**PRAYER:** *Heavenly Father thank you for your lovingkindness towards me. Thank you for reminding me of who you are and your almighty power. Thank you for the spirit of wisdom to discern the things that are you and of you. Thank you for your Holy Spirit getting me back on track when I allow the cares of this world to cause me to doubt your almighty power. For I know that with every gift you have given me comes with a responsibility to multiply it in the Earth, and as I accept that responsibility I accept your guidance and strength to accomplish it. Continue to complete a work in me. Thy will be done in me as it is in heaven, In Jesus' name, Amen.*

## Reflection and Reaction

Money may be a legitimate hindrance to your dreams, however it should not be an excuse that causes disobedience.

What do you have?

Examine your non-monetary gifts: time, skills, talents, etc.

Freely were they given and freely shall you use them.

# 42

# No Condemnation in God

*Just as He chose us in Him before the foundation of the world, that we should be holy and without blame before Him in love*
*Ephesians 1:4*

*You have forgiven the iniquity of Your people; You have covered all their sin.*
*Psalm 85:2*

*Therefore, having been justified by faith, we have peace with God through our Lord Jesus Christ, through whom also we have access by faith into this grace in which we stand, and rejoice in hope of the glory of God.*
*Romans 5: 1-2*

*There is therefore now no condemnation to those who are in Christ Jesus, who do not walk according to the flesh, but according to the Spirit.*
*Romans 8:1*

Do we truly know the definition of unconditional love? Perhaps the problem is not in the definition. Do we accept God's unconditional love? Better yet, do we know how to walk in that unconditional love? As women we tend to be harder on ourselves than we need to be. We are our own worst critics. Whenever something goes wrong we quickly blame ourselves. However we like to call it "accepting responsibility." After all, it is the "adult" thing to do. But where accepting responsibility goes wrong is in the self-punishing and the inability to move forward.

There is no condemnation in God. Once God forgives us, the act is thrown into a sea of forgetfulness. Jesus died on the cross so that we would not have to pay for our sins. To constantly punish ourselves or to continue to ask for forgiveness over and over is to crucify Him again. We can learn how to forgive others, but it is extremely difficult to forgive ourselves. We ponder over why we made the mistake rather than accepting our humaneness and moving on. Your mistake did not catch God by surprise. It did not cancel His plan for your life. Blaming or punishing yourself hinders you more than it helps you. You are unable to be used by God until you realize He can use your mistake to help someone else.

Before God created the world. He was thinking of you. He created the Earth to be our playground. It is time to come out and play! God's love sees no fault. He only sees His creation, His ability, and His purpose. We can only fathom the width and depth of His love. His desire is to see you accept His creation. Accept it. You can't change it or alter it, no matter how bad you think you messed up or how bad your heart is broken. You look at your short comings but God sees your upcoming. Stop dwelling on your mistakes. Stop blaming yourself, it is a trick of the enemy to keep you stagnant. Open you spiritual eyes and see what the Lord has in store for you.

**PRAYER:** *Heavenly Father, I thank you for your forgiveness. I thank you for your lovingkindness towards me. I ask that my eyes of understanding are enlightened that I may see your goodness. Help me to forgive myself and walk in your victory. Teach me how to let go of my past and allow you to guide me to my future in you. Thank you for choosing me to do your will, help me to accept your choice and walk in your love. In Jesus' name, Amen.*

## Reflection and Reaction

Condemnation manifests in regret.

Do you regret somethings you have said or done? Do you still talk about it or cry about it?

Are you still punishing yourself or feel that you are being punished by God?

Say out loud: "I Forgive You", say it over and over until it resonates in your spirit and you believe it. God has already forgiven you, it's time to forgive yourself.

# 43

# Confident Approach

*Now this is the confidence that we have in Him, that if we ask anything according to His will, He hears us. And if we know that He hears us, whatever we ask, we know that we have the petitions that we have asked of Him.*
*1 John 5: 14-15*

*Being confident in this very thing, that He who has begun a good work in you will complete it until the day of Jesus Christ.*
*Philippians 1: 6*

*The Lord will be your confidence and keep your foot from being caught.*
*Proverbs 3: 26*

*Therefore I rejoice that I have confidence in you in everything.*
*2 Corinthians 7: 16*

*Most assuredly, I say to you, he who believes in Me, the works that I do he will do also; and greater works than these he will do, because I go to My Father.*
*John 14:12*

We are told to have confidence in ourselves, our abilities, our talents, etc. Which I agree, someone with low self-esteem can't achieve much. But self-esteem is learned. You are not born with it. It can be nurtured by loving parents, through words of affirmation. It can also be damaged by bad people through words of defamation and bullying. Some may even say that self-esteem can be unstable. There are times and situations in which it is high, based on accomplishments and there are times and situations in which it can be low, based on disappointments or bad experiences. So then how can we rely on something so unbalanced and dependent upon feelings to be our guide for life? We cannot.

This is not the abundant living that Jesus came for. We are to have confidence in Him: the one in whose image we were created, was sent for us, died for us, and rose for us. The one who declared us righteous, prosperous, healed, delivered, blessed, above and not beneath, a lender and not a borrower, the head and not the tail, more than a conqueror…I could go on and on. We are to have confidence in knowing that He who declared us all these things, will surely perform it.

It is His will to give us all that He declared for us in His word. So why do we waste time wallowing in defeat, drowning in sorrow, begging for what God has already given and declared? Lack of confidence. We are consumed by what we see: mounting debt, loved ones passed away, good friends lost, dead end jobs, mediocre lifestyles, sickness, etc. The word declares that "Faith is the substance of things hoped for and the evidence of things not seen." Faith is required to activate the blessings of God in your life. Regardless of what it looks like, declare what thus says the Lord anyhow. Regardless of what you feel like, hold your shoulders back, and declare "My God is Bigger!" Increase your faith, know that He hears you, and know that you can have what He says you can have.

**PRAYER:** *Father God, Thank you for your favor manifesting in my life. I thank you that He that is in me is greater than He that is in the world. I am prosperous, I am blessed, I am a lender and not a borrower, I am above and not beneath. All things are working together for my good. Abundant life is available to me now and I receive it. In Jesus' name, Amen.*

**Reflection and Reaction**

Do you lack confidence in your ability to fulfill the purpose on your life?

Build your confidence by surrounding yourself with positivity and eliminating negativity. Are the people you hang around and the activities you engage in an accurate representation of the values and image you want to portray?

______________________________________________

______________________________________________

______________________________________________

______________________________________________

______________________________________________

______________________________________________

______________________________________________

______________________________________________

______________________________________________

______________________________________________

______________________________________________

______________________________________________

______________________________________________

______________________________________________

# 44

# Delayed Obedience

*Having made known to us the mystery of His will, according to His good pleasure which He purposed in Himself, that in the dispensation of the fullness of the times He might gather together in one all things in Christ, both which are in heaven and which are on earth—in Him.*
*Ephesians 1: 9-10*

*"Now therefore, if you will indeed obey My voice and keep My covenant, then you shall be a special treasure to Me above all people; for all the earth is Mine. And you shall be to Me a kingdom of priests and a holy nation." These are the words which you shall speak to the children of Israel.*
*Exodus 19: 5-6*

*Casting down arguments and every high thing that exalts itself against the knowledge of God, bringing every thought into captivity to the obedience of Christ, and being ready to punish all disobedience when your obedience is fulfilled.*
*2 Corinthians 10: 5-6*

*And the world is passing away, and the lust of it; but he who does the will of God abides forever.*
*1 John 2: 17*

Most feel procrastination is putting off for tomorrow what you can do today, or delayed obedience. However when it comes to the things of God, procrastination is still disobedience. Procrastination says to God that His timing is not important, you will do it when you get ready. Procrastination, says "I fully understand what needs to be done but I just don't want to do it right now. I'll get to it later." How can we expect the things of God, but not be willing to follow his explicit instructions?

His will or plan for you is not mystery. It has been revealed and you understand. All blessings from God come with an appointed time and season. At the appointed time Heaven and Earth will allow for all blessings (with your name on it) to come forth in Christ. This is called divine order. With divine order comes divine instruction. You must do what God says, when He says it. Don't allow procrastination to cause you to miss the move of God. Who knows when it will come again?

Obedience keeps things on track. Procrastination makes time stand still. People proclaim to be waiting on God. When God may be waiting on them to complete a task. The root of procrastination is fear: fear of failure. The steps of a good man are ordered by God, there is no failure in God. We must learn to bind fear and send it back to the pit of hell where it came from. We have victory in Jesus, all we have to do is remember He will never leave us nor forsake us.

**PRAYER:** *Heavenly Father, thank you for your mercy and grace towards me. Thank you for patiently waiting on me. Help me to heed your voice and quicken to your instructions. Procrastination and fear are not of you and I bind them both in the name of Jesus. Thank you for loving me and calling me for a purpose such as this. Help me to remember it is not about me but about your kingdom. In Jesus' name, Amen.*

## Reflection and Reaction

Has procrastination become a regular part of your life?
Do you normally put things off till the last minute claiming to work well under pressure?

Ask God to reveal the root of your delays.

# 45

# Greatness is Serving

*"Yet it shall not be so among you; but whoever desires to become great among you, let him be your servant. And whoever desires to be first among you, let him be your slave – just as the Son of Man did not come to be served, but to serve, and to give His life a ransom for many."*
*Matthew 20: 26-28*

*You are the light of [Christ to] the world. A city set on a hill cannot be hidden; nor does anyone light a lamp and put it under a basket, but on a lampstand, and it gives light to all who are in the house. Let your light shine before men in such a way that they may see your good deeds and moral excellence and [recognize and honor and] glorify your Father who is in heaven.*
*Matthew 5: 14-16 (AMP)*

*This is what the Lord, your Redeemer, the Holy One of Israel says, "I am the Lord your God, who teaches you to profit (benefit), who leads you in the way that you should go."*
*Isaiah 48:17(AMP)*

Why do you want to be successful? To provide for yourself and your family. To become your own boss. To live a comfortable lifestyle. To become rich or wealthy. To be the envy of your friends. To quiet the haters or naysayers. To come out of poverty or stop living pay check to pay check? There are many good reasons. But Jesus called us to be servants. Our purpose, our gifts and gifting, are not for us. They are for the benefit of the kingdom. They are to edify the body of saints.

To serve we must put others first. To serve we must put our own motives and intentions, regardless of how noble they are, to the side. We must put the salvation and fullness of joy in knowing the love of Christ, of others first. We serve God and in turn He teaches us how to serve others with our gifts.

To serve we must put our efforts, time, and energy into pleasing the giver. We must stay focused on God, rather than the troubles before us. Proverbs 18:6 tells us "A man's gift makes room for him and brings him before great men." Your gift is the key, not you. It is not about you but about what you have that others need. Once the need is discovered, God will show you how to use your gift to meet the need. Above all you are a servant. Serve others using the gift, don't attempt to use your gift solely for personal gain, doing so leads to failure. Doing so also limits the power of God in your life, and you will be unable to see or receive the fullness of His glory.

**PRAYER:** *Father God in the name of Jesus, thank you for gifting me to be a helpmate to your people. Help me to remember that I am your servant and I am called to serve your Kingdom. Help me to remember that it is your will and not my will that needs to be implemented in the Earth. Thank you for being my provider. Thank you for supplying all my needs. I am grateful that you are always mindful of me and in you I am lacking nothing. I surrender and allow you complete control. In Jesus' name, Amen.*

**Reflection and Reaction**

Prosperity is not a sin. But anything you put before Christ will not work. Seek to serve others through your gift and God will ensure you have all you need and more.

What need does your gift answer?

# 46

# In the Midst of Distress

*As the deer pants for the water brooks, so pants my soul for You, O God. My soul thirsts for God, for the living God. When shall I come and appear before God? My tears have been my food day and night, while they continually say to me, "Where is your God?"*
*Psalm 42:1-3*

*Why are you cast down, O my soul? And why are you so disquieted within me? Hope in God, for I shall yet praise in Him for the help of His countenance.*
*Psalm 42: 5*

*We are hard pressed on every side, yet not crushed; we are perplexed, but not in despair; persecuted, but not forsaken; struck down, but not destroyed.*
*2 Corinthians 4: 8-9*

*I will lift up my eyes to the hills- from whence comes my help? My help comes from the Lord, who made heaven and earth.*
*Psalm 121: 1-2*

There are things and situations that come at us sometimes that knock us down and leave us, literally speechless. These times consume us so that we feel that God is missing or has left us. Tears stain our pillows as we long for His touch and comfort. Our hearts feel empty, our ears are stopped up, and we feel physically deaf. All we are able to hear is the taunting of the enemy saying "Where is your God?"

Momentary deafness causes us to rely on memory. The beauty of His touch. The joy of His presence. The awesomeness of His power. His faithfulness. The perfect timing of His blessings. We remember when our hearts were full. We remember how excited we were when He saved us, when He poured out His love for us, when He set us free from our pasts, when He delivered us from the pain of our hurts, when he healed us from sickness and disease, when He saved our loved ones, protected our children, provided for our family, all just because He loved us. We reflect on His glory, His unmerited favor and pant after Him. Because if we could just touch the hem of His garment we know that we will be made whole again.

In a temporary impairment of tongue, we muster up enough strength to say Thank you. Thank Him for always being with us. We love Him anyway. Despite what it feels like, despite what it looks like, we love Him anyway. We can't see it now. But we wait with expectations, and know that we are still in His will and His presence. In His presence is fullness of joy. Joy produces confidence. We may not see it. We may not feel it, but God is working things out. We expect and serve a living God. Our God can see. Our God can hear. Our God can do.

**PRAYER:** *Heavenly Father thank you. Thank you for being my comforter, my provider, my source and my shield in times of trouble. Thank you for never leaving me or forsaking me. I thank you, for bringing to my remembrance your faithfulness and lovingkindness towards me. Your word* *says weeping may endure for a night but joy comes in the morning. Thank you for joy. I thank you that though it may not feel good at this moment, I know with certainty and confidence that you are always with me. I praise you in advance for the testimony. In Jesus' name, Amen.*

**Reflection and Reaction**

The storm can be difficult, but our ability to stand/to weather the storm, is contingent upon our remembrance of God's faithfulness.

Reflect on what He did yesterday, today and His promises for tomorrow.

# 47

# Would You Like That Super-Sized?

*May the Lord God of your fathers make you a thousand times more numerous than you are, and bless you as He promised you.*
*Deuteronomy 1: 11*

*And I am come down to deliver them out of the hand of the Egyptians, and to bring them up out of that land unto a good land and a large land, unto a land flowing with milk and honey; unto the place of the Canaanites, and the Hittites, and the Amorites, and the Perizzites, and the Hivites, and the Jebusites.*
*Exodus 3:8 (KJV)*

*For my thoughts are not your thoughts, neither are your ways my ways, saith the LORD. For as the heavens are higher than the earth, so are my ways higher than your ways, and my thoughts than your thoughts. For as the rain cometh down, and the snow from heaven, and returneth not thither, but watereth the earth, and maketh it bring forth and bud, that it may give seed to the sower, and bread to the eater: So shall my word be that goeth forth out of my mouth: it shall not return unto me void, but it shall accomplish that which I please, and it shall prosper in the thing whereto I sent it.*
*Isaiah 55: 8-11 (KJV)*

There is nothing wrong with taking time to stop and smell the roses. God is an awesome God. He has done great things in our lives. We have an awesome testimony. In times of trouble, we reflect on these times and gain strength and are encouraged to hold on, as we know our help is on the way. With each goal we set before God, we are to say thank you, and celebrate the great accomplishments. However we should not stop there. We are to be happy in all things, we are to be content in whatever state we are in, but we are not to settle in mediocrity.

Our God is Big. No He is Bigger than Big. He did not come for us to live in mediocrity. To settle for "just enough." It is not enough to get out of debt. God wants you to cancel the debt of others. It is not enough to pay your house off, God wants you to pay somebody else's house off. It is not enough for you to get a promotion at work, God wants you to run the company. It is not enough to get out of poverty, God wants you to bring others out with you. It is not enough for you to go further than your parents, God wants you to outdo multiple generations. We are to go from glory to glory to glory. Don't get stuck in one glory.

Would you like that super-sized? Would you like to experience God-sized dreams? Our dreams are small compared to what He has in store. Are you willing to do what it takes to get it? You can't TRY God out, you must TRUST Him out. Trust Him out of poverty. Trust Him out of debt. Trust Him out of mediocrity. Grab hold to His hand and allow Him to lead you into a large land flowing with milk and honey. A land you never thought was possible or even existed. Surrender and watch God work.

**PRAYER:** *Heavenly Father thank you for all that you have done, are doing and going to do in my life. I surrender today, my will and my plans. Thy will be done in my life, have your way in me. Help me to trust you* *and not rely on or worry about what I see. Open my spiritual eyes that I may see the blessings you have in store for me. Thank you for leading me in the path of your righteousness. In Jesus' name, Amen.*

**Reflection and Reaction**

What are your biggest dreams?

No matter how big they are, they are not bigger than what God has in store.

How can you begin to trust Him out?

# 48

# How Soon We Forget

*I remember you, the kindness of your youth, the love of your betrothal, when you went after Me in the wilderness, in a land not sown.*
*Jeremiah 2:2b*

*But seek first the kingdom of God and His righteousness and all these things shall be added to you.*
*Matthew 6:33*

*The Lord is not slack concerning His promise, as some count slackness, but is longsuffering toward us, not willing that any should perish but that all should come to repentance.*
*2 Peter 3: 9*

*Knowing that the testing of your faith produces patience. But let patience have its perfect work, that you may be perfect and complete, lacking nothing.*
*James 1: 3- 4*

What's your salvation story? Do you remember what it felt like when you first got saved? Or perhaps how you felt when you experienced true repentance and forgiveness and decided to follow Jesus? You were at church every time the doors swung open; bible study, Sunday school, morning service, evening service, revival, this meeting and that meeting. How you were communing with God and He was communing with you. How you felt like His favorite, because God was blessing you with things that crossed your mind without asking. How soon we forget!

Israel had forgotten what the Lord had done for them, bringing them out of bondage, and began to slip back into their old ways. This is what we do when we begin to murmur and complain about what we don't have. We allow our desires, or our temporary need, to overshadow His love for us and His perfect will to be done in us. O ye ungrateful children. How can we have everything we need, yet focus on the one thing we want and feel deprived and forsaken? How soon we forget!

The Lord does not come to our pity parties. Complaining prevents us from hearing from God and prolongs our forward progress. So "Man Up" or put your "Big Girl Panties" on. God has such big plans for us. Part of praising God is in recognizing and giving thanks for all He has done. Praise impels Him to do more. Don't let anyone, including yourself, prevent you from being all that God wants you to be. So what if you don't have what you want when you want it, Praise Him Anyway.

**PRAYER:** *Heavenly Father, thank you for all you have done for me. Forgive me for being ungrateful and forgetting how far I have come. I thank you for all the victories thus far. I understand that though it may seem rough now, trials come to make me strong. For you said in your word that* *in due season I shall reap if I faint not. Thank you for teaching me patience, for I know that in the end I shall count it all joy. In Jesus' name, Amen.*

(Today's devotional is an excerpt from my book *Stop Asking Me Why Am I Single*)

**Reflection and Reaction**

Have you forgotten how good God has been?

Have you allowed your desires to distract you and present you from praising God?

What can you do to get back to your first love?

_______________________________________________

_______________________________________________

_______________________________________________

_______________________________________________

_______________________________________________

_______________________________________________

_______________________________________________

_______________________________________________

_______________________________________________

_______________________________________________

_______________________________________________

_______________________________________________

_______________________________________________

_______________________________________________

_______________________________________________

# 49

# At His Word

*And Elijah the Tishbite, who was of the inhabitants of Gilead, said unto Ahab, As the LORD God of Israel liveth, before whom I stand, there shall not be dew nor rain these years, but according to my word. And the word of the LORD came unto him, saying, get thee hence, and turn thee eastward, and hide thyself by the brook Cherith,that is before Jordan. And it shall be, that thou shalt drink of the brook; and I have commanded the ravens to feed thee there. So he went and did according unto the word of the LORD: for he went and dwelt by the brook Cherith,that is before Jordan. And the ravens brought him bread and flesh in the morning, and bread and flesh in the evening; and he drank of the brook. And it came to pass after a while, that the brook dried up, because there had been no rain in the land. And the word of the LORD came unto him, saying, arise, get thee to Zarephath, which belongeth to Zidon, and dwell there: behold, I have commanded a widow woman there to sustain thee. So he arose and went to Zarephath. And when he came to the gate of the city, behold, the widow woman was there gathering of sticks: and he called to her, and said, fetch me, I pray thee, a little water in a vessel, that I may drink. And as she was going to fetch it, he called to her, and said, bring me, I pray thee, a morsel of bread in thine hand. And she said, As the LORD thy God liveth, I have not a cake, but an handful of meal in a barrel, and a little oil in a cruse: and, behold, I am gathering two sticks, that I may go in and dress it for me and my son, that we may eat it, and die. And Elijah said unto her, Fear not; go and do as thou hast said: but make me thereof a little cake first, and bring it unto me, and after make for thee and for thy son. For thus saith the LORD God of Israel, The barrel of meal shall not waste, neither shall the cruse of oil fail, until the day that the LORD sendeth rain upon the earth. And she went and did according to the saying of Elijah: and she, and he, and her house, did eat many days. And the barrel of meal wasted not, neither did the cruse of oil fail, according to the word of the LORD, which he spake by Elijah.*

*1 Kings 17: 1-16 (KJV)*

The way of the world is self-preservation. But the law of God is faith. Even in the midst of trouble we must stand on His word. Elijah was obedient. He didn't leave before the brook dried up. Though there had to have been signs. I'm sure he saw the flow of water stop. I'm sure he saw water turn to mud, and mud turn to dry land. He may have questioned why God left him there to die. But he waited on the Word.

On the other hand, I'm sure Elijah was comfortable, enjoying the blessings of God. God commanded an unclean bird to bring him bread and meat in the morning and evening. He was sipping water at the brook. Life was good. Yes God promised a drought, but things were going so well, maybe God changed His mind. But the drought came. We cannot get too complacent in one place that we procrastinate when God says go to another place. At His word we are to obey.

God has ways to bless us that we haven't even thought about. However we must slow down and see, don't move too fast, as we may overlook them. What if Elijah had left before the brook dried up? Would the widow woman have received him? We have to do what God says. Don't try to out think or get ahead of God. Stay at the brook. Stay with the word, until He gives you another word. Stay where you heard the Lord say stay. Do what you heard the Lord say do. Remember it is not all about you. Don't try to help God out. Your blessings are not just about you. God wants to set you up so that you may bless others. God is teaching you how to live and depend on Him; when you do, He has unconventional ways to bless you. Trust Him and see.

**PRAYER:** *Heavenly Father, thank you for providing for me. Thank you for your guidance. Help me to be patient and wait on you. Help me to stand on your word. Regardless of what I see, help me to remember that* *you are not slack concerning me. You are not a liar and your word shall not return to you void. Fill me with your strength to endure till the end, so that your glory may be revealed in me. In Jesus' name, Amen.*

**Reflection and Reaction**

Do you trust God at His word?

Have you gotten impatience waiting for the next set of instructions?

Keep doing what He told you to do until He tell you to do something different.

# 50

# Be Strong in the Lord

*Finally, my brethren, be strong in the Lord and in the power of his might. Put on the whole armor of God, that ye may be able to stand against the wiles of the devil. For we wrestle not against flesh and blood, but against principalities, against powers, against the rulers of the darkness of this world, against spiritual wickedness in high places.*
*Ephesians 6: 10-12 (KJV)*

Selfish ambition can sometimes get the best of us. We spend so much time perfecting our crafts. Tending to the needs of our families and ourselves. Or calculating how much time to allot for extracurricular activities. Then life happens, someone dies, someone takes ill, jobs are lost, marriages fail, children are born, promotions on the job, increase in responsibilities, etc. and suddenly our world is limited to a square. We feel all alone. The anxiety takes its toll and we began to lose sleep. Wake up with bad attitudes. The enemy has crept in like a thief in the night. We are so consumed with our own issues that we didn't even know we left the door open. Yes, in all the turmoil, in all the ups and downs, we forgot to pray.

Each day we forget to say thank you Lord. Each day we forget to bask in His presence. Each day we forget to read and study His word. Each day we forget to pray. We open the door for the enemy to come in a wreak havoc. This life of a Christian is not for the weak. God never promised us a bed of roses. In fact He guaranteed trials and tribulations would come. But He also promised that if we delighted in Him, if we trusted in Him, if we abided in Him, if we called on Him, He would come to us in our time of need, give us the desires of our heart and direct our paths.

We battle not against flesh and blood but against principalities. We are fully equipped with everything that pertains to Godliness, not to rest when things are good, but to do battle. The enemy does not take a break, he does not slack up. Be strong in the Lord. Commune with Him through reading His word. Take time to bask in His presence by proclaiming who He is in your life. Don't slack up, stay in the fight. Petition the throne with confidence knowing your requests are being heard. Give Him no rest until He performs the word He has spoken. In the meantime, things will happen but Be Strong and Be Faithful for He who is in you is always faithful.

**PRAYER:** *Lord thank you for your faithfulness and kindness towards me. Thank you for reminding me that you are mighty in battle and the victory is already won. Help me to remember that my best weapon in warfare is prayer and communing with you. Remind me of my date with you. I thank you for giving me peace and for being my strength and joy. In Jesus' name, Amen.*

## Reflection and Reaction

Do you pray daily? Do you read your word daily? What hinders your commune time?

Set your alarm clock a few minutes early, listen to the bible on cd at work; find a way to stay in His presence by communing with Him daily.

# 51

# Do You Really Believe?

*God is not a man, that he should lie; neither the son of man, that he should repent: hath he said, and shall he not do it? Or hath he spoken, and shall he not make it good?*
*Numbers 23:19 (KJV)*

*Death and life are in the power of the tongue: and they that love it shall eat the fruit thereof.*
*Proverbs 18: 21(KJV)*

*For verily I say unto you, That whosoever shall say unto this mountain, Be thou removed, and be thou cast into the sea; and shall not doubt in his heart, but shall believe that those things which he saith shall come to pass; he shall have whatsoever he saith.*
*Mark 11: 23 (KJV)*

We know that God can do anything and everything. But do we believe that everything is available and accessible to us? Salvation is NOT free. It requires your belief. Belief that God sent Jesus to die on the cross for our sins. Belief that our sins are forgiven and cast into the sea of forgetfulness. Belief in the impossible. In addition, belief also requires faith. Faith in what we cannot see. Faith that, though times are rough, God is always working, always in control, and always thinking of us. Faith requires action. His word tells us that faith without works is dead. What have you allowed to die?

His word teaches us that life and death is in the power of the tongue. Our words are spirit and life. What have you spoken over your situation? Constant complaining about how things are bad or how you have such bad luck only causes your situation to magnify, you gave it life and you can end its life. Stop going to the wake and walking around the situation, crying, begging, pleading, moaning, asking "why Lord." It's time to bury that thang, "ashes to ashes, dust to dust."

God called us to speak to our mountain, not stand there and look at, or even to walk around it. Speak to it and it shall be removed. If you don't know what to say, then there lies a deeper problem. The enemy can only be silenced with the word. In times of trouble, you don't have time to go grab your bible, fumble through it and find a scripture. You must study the word daily, so that in times of distress, the Holy Spirit can bring to your remembrance an on time word applicable to the situation at hand.

Stop soliciting prayers from others. You don't know how they are living, their prayers may not go further than the ceiling. Encourage yourself, speak over yourself. You have the best mediator, Jesus Christ, petitioning your Father on your behalf. Work the word and it shall work for you. God's word will not return to Him void.

**PRAYER:** *Dear Heavenly Father, thank you for being my everything. I believe every word you have spoken over my life. As I grow in you and with you, help my unbelief. Help me to come before you boldly. Help me to speak to any situation that comes my way. Help me to trust that once I give it to you, you are working it out on my behalf. I acknowledge your power and authority in my life and submit my ways to your ways. I acknowledge I need you to lead and guide me into all truths. Thy will be done. In Jesus' name, Amen.*

## Reflection and Reaction

What promise has God made to you? Do you have a hard time believing?

Belief allows us to approach the throne boldly and speak boldly in times of despair. Strengthen your belief by reading and applying the word daily.

________________________________________

________________________________________

________________________________________

________________________________________

________________________________________

________________________________________

________________________________________

________________________________________

________________________________________

________________________________________

# 52

# Fighting Change

*"By faith Abraham obeyed when he was called to go out to a place that he was to receive as an inheritance. And he went out, not knowing where he was going."*
*Hebrews 11: 8 (ESV)*

*Daniel answered and said: "Blessed be the name of God forever and ever, for wisdom and might are His. And He changes the times and the seasons; He removes kings and raises up kings; He gives wisdom to the wise and knowledge to those who have understanding. He reveals deep and secret things; He knows what is in the darkness, and light dwells with Him*
*Daniel 2: 20-22*

*"Do not be conformed to this world, but be transformed by the renewal of your mind, that by testing you may discern what is the will of God, what is good and acceptable and perfect."*
*Romans 12: 2 (ESV)*

*"And we all, with unveiled face, beholding the glory of the Lord, are being transformed into the same image from one degree of glory to another. For this comes from the Lord who is the Spirit."*
*2 Corinthians 3: 18 (ESV)*

We spend our entire lives fighting change. Day changes to night. We invented daylight savings time to make the days longer. Winter changes to summer and vice versa. We invented air conditioning and heat. Eventually the young will become old. We invented anti-aging cream, Botox, etc. When will we learn that change is inevitable to create growth? No matter what we invent, no matter how we try to fight change. The one thing we cannot change is time. Whether springing forward an hour or falling back an hour, the hour missed or gained is never recovered. Heat and air may keep us cool or warm on the inside, but the moment we step outside, into reality, that which we were trying to escape slaps us in the face. And no amount of aging cream, Botox treatments or liposuctions will give us back the years we are trying to erase. Rather than fight change, we should embrace it and the blessings that come with it.

Marriages fail because people say "He/She changed." Well yeah, as we grow and mature we are supposed to change. People continue to live in mediocrity, stuck in poverty, because they refuse to try something new and live outside the box. No matter how much experience one has, when you enter into a new job, you must be trained on the way things are done in the new company or positions. With change comes blessings. New ideas are generated with change. Creativity is sparked with change. Your inability to move to the next level is due to your inability to accept change. Yes God does not change, He is the same today and forever more. However as we change, His methods change…We are God in the Earth. God moves through people.

Change is scary. It requires you to trust in the Creator. It requires you to be teachable. It requires faith. Faith that if God brought you to it. If God put it in you. He will bring you through it. He will help you do it. You are more than capable.

Embrace change and embrace the abundant life freely given to you by your Creator.

**PRAYER:** *Heavenly Father, thank you for endowing me with the ability and willingness to change. As I embrace change, help me to remain teachable and humble as to not miss the wisdom in learning. Let your glory be revealed in me. Thy will be done in my life. In Jesus' name, Amen.*

**Reflection and Reaction**

Are you fighting change? Yet still wondering why nothing is changing in your life. Ask God what He wants to teach you, embrace the change knowing that God is with you every step of the way.

# 53

# By His Spirit

*So he answered and said to me: "This is the word of the Lord to Zerubbabel, 'Not by might nor by power, but by My Spirit,'" says the Lord of hosts.*

*Zechariah 4:6*

Patience shall be your virtue. Stop trying to fix it. Stop trying to plan your own way. Heed God's voice, heed His directions, and you shall see His glory. Yes faith without works is dead, but there will come a time, when God wants you to DO nothing, except watch. Watch His hand. He is not slow and His timing is perfect. Where you go, you must learn to not only survive but to thrive. You thrive by allowing God to work. Let God be God. Let Him be YOUR God. Sit back and watch His plan unfold.

The difference between surviving and thriving is: He who has control, controls the outcome. Survivors control their outcome, they barely make it because they can only control what they see. Their planning can only solve the immediate issue. Those who thrive relinquish control to God, His presence, and His guidance because God is able to see what they cannot. He commands the unseen. Survivors have just enough to make it, while those who thrive have more than enough (blessing them and others).

He who has the greater vision, has the greater test as well as the greater reward.

**PRAYER:** *Dear Heavenly Father, thank you for supplying all my needs. Your word says your promises are yea and Amen. Your word says your word will not return to you void. Help me to be patient and wait on you. I relinquish control to you and submit to your will being fulfilled in my life. Thank you for your faithfulness. In Jesus' name, Amen.*

**Reflection and Reaction**

Are you still operating in survival mode? What action can you implement today to begin to thrive?

Trust God to lead you by His Spirit.

# 54

# Prepared People

*"Thus says the Lord of hosts: 'In those days ten men from every language of the nations shall grasp the sleeve of a Jewish man, saying "let us go with you, for we have heard that God is with you.' "*

*Zechariah 8:23*

You do not have to beg or try to convince people to believe in your dream or your vision. You do not need as much help as you think. God is with you. His glory is upon you. Your light is shining brightly. When you try to convince others, it is out of selfish gain or ambition. People will want to go with you because they can see God's light. God has already prepared them. They are waiting for you. As you go, you will meet them, you will know them, and you will know He has sent them.

Success is all over you. Believe in you, you are well equipped. Believe in God. He will not allow you to fail. Stop worrying. Worrying drowns out God's voice and causes doubt. You are frustrated because you are trying to figure out His plan. Which again causes you to doubt his instructions, because they are not what you imagined. As you go, you will see God's plan unfolding. As you go, you will gain a better understanding. Trust Him. Go when He says go. Do when He says do. Your gift has made room for you and is leading you into the presence of great men.

**PRAYER:** *Heavenly Father, thank you for ordering my steps. Thank you for divine connections. Thank you for placing people in my paths who want to bless me and not hinder me. Thank you for the gift that you have placed in me and for allowing me the opportunity to use them for your kingdom. Help me to decrease that you may increase. I bind the hands of the enemy that brings about worry and distraction now and replace it with confidence in your word and your promises. In Jesus' name, Amen.*

**Reflection and Reaction**

Do you waste time searching for support or people to buy into you gift? Rather than attempting to make people follow you, ask God to lead you to the people who He has prepared for you.

# 55

# Well Faith

*Saying, "What do you want Me to do for you?" He said, "Lord that I may receive my sight." Then Jesus said to him, "Receive your sight; your faith has made you well."*

*Luke 18: 41-42*

Your faith has made you well.

Your faith will make you well.

Your faith will keep you in perfect peace.

Your faith will keep you strong.

Your faith will keep you from worrying.

'Well Faith" is confidence in God. Confidence that He is able. Confidence that He will do all that He has promised. Confidence that His timing is perfect. Confidence that His plan is perfect.

"Well Faith" is assurance in God. Unwavering, unshakeable, assurance that God has already done it! It is just a matter of time for it to be manifested in the earth.

Trust God and lean not on your own understanding. Don't allow your right now frustrations to dictate your actions thus causing you to react out of God's will. Sometimes we don't understand why we are alone in the journey. God does this to keep us from messing up. Other people can influence you to doubt God and do things according to worldly customs. God's ways will not adhere to societal norms.

You shall have no lack, if you trust and follow God.

**PRAYER:** *Heavenly Father, thank you for your faithfulness. Help me to stand in my faith. Help me to rely on you and not my own understanding. Help me to acknowledge you in all my ways. Thank you for your supernatural strength and thank you for keeping me in perfect peace. In Jesus' name, Amen.*

## Reflection and Reaction

Do you practice "Well Faith"? Cast your worries and concerns on Him and thank Him for working it out in your favor.

# 56

# Stop and Smell the Roses

*So I perceived that nothing is better than that a man should rejoice in his own works, for that is his heritage. For who can bring him to see what will happen after him?*

*Ecclesiastes 3:22*

Take time to rejoice in how far you have come and where you have been. Doing so reflects a heart of gratefulness. Remember in the Old Testament, every time God did something for His people, they responded by building an altar in that place as a reminder of the goodness of God. Today we don't build altars but we can do so by remembering and reflecting on the faithfulness and goodness of God. Doing so not only expresses gratitude but is also assurance that God can do even greater works.

There is no better preparation for tomorrow than yesterday and today. Though yesterday is gone, since you have been given another day, reflect on yesterday and use today to make corrections. This will prevent you from duplicating mistakes while also helping you capitalize on successes.

Don't waste today worried about tomorrow. For today then becomes unproductive. A wasted today leads to a busy tomorrow. God is with you today. Acknowledge Him. Thank Him and allow Him to order your steps.

**PRAYER:** *Heavenly Father, thank you for all that you have done and all that you are going to do in the future. Help me to remember the joys of yesterday, focus on today and not be worried about tomorrow. Thank you for your word as a reminder that you are always with me and are always mindful of me. In Jesus' name, Amen.*

## Reflection and Reaction

Make time for daily or weekly reflection.

What transpired in this past week? What are your successes? Celebrate them. What could be done better? Implement a plan for improvement or hire someone!

# 57

# Less is Better

*Do not be rash with your mouth, and let not your heart utter anything hastily before God. For God is in heaven and you on earth; therefore let your words be few.*

*Ecclesiastes 5:2*

It is better to say nothing than to speak negatively. This includes your thoughts and random conversations. Times maybe tough, but what you say could be prolonging your wait. Take it to the Lord in prayer. Don't allow yourself to have a pity party, spilling your guts to anyone who will listen. When you are believing God for a specific situation, have one or two persons (your prayer warriors) who you can vent to or confide in. Otherwise keep your mouth shut. Let "God is working it out" be your proclamation to all who inquire.

God sees all and knows all. He is teaching you to trust him. Don't allow the negativity of what could be or should be affect the reality of his promises. Negative thoughts and conversations corrode your faith and block His communication. You cannot hear God because you are thinking too much and doing too much.

Remember regardless of whether others tell you or not, people are watching you. Blessings and curses cannot spring from the same well. You may be the only God someone sees. You may be that example of faith that someone needs. Remember your quiet place. Meet God there daily, He wants to be alone with you. Quiet your thoughts. God is still with you. His promises are still true. He has not forgotten you. Faith is all that is required of you. Stand and when you have done all else, stand some more!

**PRAYER:** *Heavenly Father, though the storm is raging help me to remember that you are with me. Though I have yet to see your promises help me to remember that you are not a liar and what you have promised shall come to past. Thank you for those people you have placed in my life to pray me through. Thank you, for your word says when I am weak you are strong. May your peace and your strength give me the power to stand. In Jesus' name, Amen.*

**Reflection and Reaction**

Examine your past week: How much negativity have you surrounded yourself with? How has it affected your mood, your time and your actions?

# 58

# Wavering Faith

*And it came to pass, when he was close to entering Egypt, that he said to Sarai his wife, "Indeed I know that you are a woman of beautiful countenance. Therefore it will happen, when the Egyptians see you, that they will say, 'This is his wife', and they will kill me, but they will let you live. Please say you are my sister, that it may be well with me for your sake, and that I may live because of you."*

*Genesis 12: 11-13*

Wavering faith is not the same as weak faith. Faith has three parts:

1. You will be tested. Testing does not mean you have done something wrong, are doing something wrong, or have fallen off track. It just means there are things you must go through on the journey. Stop punishing yourself. God is still well pleased. He is still working on your behalf.
2. There will be an uncovering. Faith will let you know what you are made of. It will expose your weaknesses and your strengths. This exposition does not necessarily require action on your part. Just because you become weak in the wait does not mean something has to be corrected or done before you can get your promise. Stop seeing God as only a God of consequences. You will not be punished for every mistake. Remember He knows what you will do before you do it anyway, yet He still made the promise.
3. God's faithfulness is sufficient. Even when you mess up God has your back. Trust that He will not let you fall. Trust that He will not renege on His word. The grace of God will keep you, if you allow Him.

**PRAYER:** *Heavenly Father thank you for your faithfulness and kindness towards me. Help me to keep my eyes on you during this time of struggles and trials. Help me to stay focused on your promises and not my current situations. Open my spiritual eyes that I may see the work of your hands. In Jesus' name, Amen.*

## Reflection and Reaction

Do you feel you are being punished because your faith is wavering?

Faith strengthens as we learn to trust Him not when we go through without error.

# 59

# Do It Afraid

*Do not be afraid of sudden terror, nor of trouble from the wicked when it comes; For the Lord will be your confidence, and will keep your foot from being caught.*

*Proverbs 3: 25-26*

*In God I have put my trust; I will not be afraid. What can man do to me?*

*Psalm 56: 11*

You know you were created for greatness. You know that there is something more, something better that you should be doing. The spirit man is anxious, but the flesh is afraid. Moving ahead pushes you into the unknown and standing still keeps you living in mediocrity.

The bible states that anything with more than one head is a monster. Fear is a monstrosity, it has multiple heads. When fear moves in he brings several friends with him.

1. Fear of the unknown – Afraid of what lies ahead
2. Fear of success – Afraid it just might work
3. Fear of failure – Afraid it might not work
4. Fear of rejection – Afraid others won't approve
5. Fear of being alone – Afraid you may have to stand alone

I can name many more, as the list is never-ending, it grows daily. One thing is for sure, fear did not come from God. We have a Father walking with us to help us fulfill His purpose. Why not Do It Afraid? Have confidence in knowing that there is no failure in God. The word of God will never lead you where the grace of God can't protect you. Trust that you are in good hands. Have confidence in knowing that God is always with you. His word promises He would never leave you. He is your protection, your comfort and your peace. Though the road may be tough, and even in the face of adversity God has the final say so. He will bless you and even your enemies will not be able to deny His presence and abilities.

Do it Afraid! What do you have to lose? God opens doors no man can shut and closes doors no man can open. What God has destined no man can erase. Trust God and watch Him perform His word. He is not a liar and His word will not return to Him void. The appointed time has come. Fear has over stayed his welcome. How long will you allow him to control you, delay your destiny, consume your thoughts, and regulate your actions? Do it Afraid!

**PRAYER**: *Heavenly Father, I admit that I have allowed fear to consume and prevent me from following your commandments and fulfilling my purpose. Help me to remember that fear is not of you and it is my obedience that will allow you control in my life. Help me to remember I have nothing to fear as you are always with me. In Jesus' name, Amen.*

## Reflection and Reaction

What are you afraid of? Fear manifests itself in many forms: doubt, procrastination, indecisiveness, anxiety, etc.

The best way to face fear is to confront it! It will not go away, use it as motivation.

______________________________________________

______________________________________________

______________________________________________

______________________________________________

______________________________________________

______________________________________________

______________________________________________

______________________________________________

______________________________________________

______________________________________________

______________________________________________

______________________________________________

______________________________________________

# 60

# Complete in Him

*Before lest anyone cheat you through philosophy and empty deceit, according to the tradition of men, according to the basic principles of the world, and not according to Christ. For in Him dwells all the fullness of the Godhead bodily; and you are complete in Him, who is head of all principality and power.*

*Colossians 2: 8-10*

When things start going south, it is easy and even justifiable for our thinking to go south as well. What have I done wrong? Why has God forsaken me? Both are questions that quickly arise when the storms of life come raging. But as second nature as it is, we have to fight for God's presence. We have to fight to remain positive. We have to fight to remember that God is still with us.

Don't get sidetracked by worldly things or doctrines. Your focus should be on Christ. As easy as it is to have a temper tantrum, to stop reading the word or to stop going to church; we have to keep our minds stayed on Christ and the things of God. The word says we are more than conquerors. The word says that all things work together for our good. But in order for it to work in our favor, we have to give it to God. We have to retain our composure and do and say according to the word. We have to keep our mind off our storms and on the promises of God. Don't worry about what you lack or what you appear to be losing. Remember you are complete in Him.

Everything you need, God is already providing. There is no lack in God. Lack only exists in impatience. Remember that God's timing is perfect. Remember that there is no good thing He will withhold from you. Remember that the storm, this storm, any storm is only temporary.

**PRAYER:** *Dear Heavenly Father, though I am troubled I thank you that you are with me. I thank you for providing all my needs. Help me to remember that with you I lack nothing. Help me to remember that I am victorious and complete in you. In Jesus' name, Amen.*

## Reflection and Reaction

Is lack one of your excuses? Write down exactly what you need.

If money, how much?

If a service, what kind?

Be specific with God and watch Him open doors.

Don't just say or assume you can't, ask for what you need to get it done.

# 61

# Wherever You Go

*This book of the Law shall not depart from your mouth, but you shall meditate in it day and night, that you may observe to do according to all that is written in it. For then you will make your way prosperous, and then you shall have good success. "Have I not commanded you? Be strong and of good courage, do not be afraid nor be dismayed, for the Lord your God is with you wherever you go."*

*Joshua 1: 8-9*

How do you expect to hear God without the word? How do you expect to obtain instructions without spending time with Him? God speaks through the word. He is the word. God and the word are not and cannot be separated. I know the world thinks it doesn't take all that or may call you "Holier than thou" but as Christians, the bible, the word and God is our blueprint for life. Purpose is discovered and once discovered it becomes a command. You are commanded to fulfill that purpose in the Earth. It does not and will not change. As you go and as you grow you may see the magnitude of God's power and vision but your purpose will not change! Regardless of what your current situation looks like. Regardless of what it feels like. Regardless of what others say. Regardless of support from others or lack thereof. You have been commanded to fulfill that purpose.

God is the way to the success you seek. In fact, success begins with Him. His way is better. Trust Him and do your part. Many people like to proclaim that they are "waiting on God" but the truth is God is waiting on them. God lives in us and His power is manifested through us. If we don't move, if we don't go, He can't move or go. God's power and anointing will never leave us however we can walk away from it. How? By allowing sin and condemning thoughts to consume us. Stop allowing your thoughts, your wants/desires, and your distorted perception of success to hold you captive. Success is not in material possession, title, riches, or political status. These things can perish at any given moment. Rather success is in doing the work of the Lord, that which you were created to do.

Don't you understand, God is with you wherever you go? Your loss, your pain, your experiences were not punishment. They were not a mistake. He allowed it to make you stronger, to push you into your destiny, to show you who He is, and to use it for His glory. If He allowed your plan to manifest, then you would believe it was your own doing, your own efforts. It's not that difficult. You are trying too hard, thinking too hard. Let go. Let God be God and you be His servant. When the time is right, you will know what to do. When you don't know what to do or are confused about the next step, it is because you trying to move ahead of God or without God.

**PRAYER**: *Dear Heavenly Father, thank you for the gifts and talents you have placed in me. I ask that you help me to be patient and wait on your instructions. Help me to remember that you are with me wherever I go. As you lead me in the right directions help me change my perception of success. Open my spiritual eyes that I may see your way and your hands at work in my life. Open my ears and my heart that I may hear your voice and heed your commands. As I wait on you, help me to consistently study your word daily and bask in your presence. In Jesus' name I pray, Amen.*

## Reflection and Reaction

There is no fast track to success. There is a process, even with God.

Are you trying to stop or abort the process?

Are you prepared for what you're asking for?

Preparation proceeds placement. Don't give in.

________________________________________

________________________________________

________________________________________

________________________________________

________________________________________

# 62

# Bystander or Participant…You Decide

*For if you remain completely silent at this time, relief and deliverance will arise for the Jews from another place but you and your father's house will perish. Yet who knows whether you have come to the kingdom for such a time as this.*

*Esther 4:14*

Esther went through a lot of preparation, with Mortdecai's help, to make it to the kingdom. She may have thought she made it on beauty or that once there she could bask in her new found wealth and status. But God allowed her favor for His purpose: to save His people.

Many times we want success for our own fulfillment: money, fame, power, etc. But we have to remember who is in control and that our thoughts are not His thoughts. Mordecai reminded Esther who she was, and that her silence could lead to her demise as well. Like Esther, we have a decision to make, because the scripture lets us know the consequences of that decision.

1. Relief and deliverance will arise. God has need of your gift. He wants you to use it to help others. However don't think that you're irreplaceable. God will not allow others to suffer because of your disobedience. We must realize that it's not just about us. Others are counting on you. Decide if you will be God's chosen vessel or watch someone else do it and get the benefits as well.
2. You and your father's house will perish. Again it's not just about you. This is your legacy! Will the dream die with you? Generations to come will benefit from your obedience. Some of us today are reaping the benefits of our parents and grandparents obedience and prayers. Will you pass down faithfulness, obedience and reliance on God or disobedience, curses and rebellion? Decide if the future of not only yourself but your children's children are worth it.
3. Yet who knows if you have come to the kingdom for such a time as this. You can't out strategize God. He carefully orchestrates every part of His will and vision for our lives. Nothing is a coincidence but rather divine

appointments and connections. Decide if you will allow Him control.

You have free will, it's your life and your decision. Remember God wants to bless us exceeding and abundantly above what we can ask or think. Don't settle for the small prize when something, not only bigger, but something you didn't know you wanted or needed awaits. Making it to the kingdom was a great accomplishment for Esther, but if she had gotten comfortable, she would have been easily replaced. However her obedience and willingness to heed Godly counsel sealed her legacy as one of the greatest Queens and not to mention there is a whole book in the bible about her!

**PRAYER:** *Dear God, thank you for choosing me for such a task as this. Help me to remember that it is not about me but for your glory that others may be blessed. I submit today to your will and plan for my life. I allow you complete control. Help me to remember that success is not in material possession but in obedience and helping others. I thank you for placing people in my life who will remind me of my purpose and assist me in my journey. In Jesus' name, Amen.*

## Reflection and Reaction

All God requires is a yes.

Are you ready to change lives?

Are you ready to impact nations?

The dream begins with you, but it is bigger than you.

Decide if you will be on the team or sitting in the stands.

# 63

# Never Alone

*And immediately, coming up from the water, He saw the heavens parting and the Spirit descending upon Him like a dove. Then a voice from heaven, "You are My beloved Son, in whom I am well pleased." Immediately the Spirit drove Him into the wilderness. And He was there in the wilderness forty days, tempted by Satan and was with the wild beasts; and the Angels ministered to Him.*

*Mark 1:10-13*

As immediately as God established Him as His son, He was immediately led in the wilderness to be tempted. Mark is saying many things in these four verses:

1. God is well pleased. The moment you accept our assignment and act on it, know that God is pleased. The heavens are parting and descending upon you like a dove. Your light is shining brightly for all those to see.
2. The Holy Spirit does not always lead us to the easiest route. It is a myth that God's direction will always be void of struggle. But know that He does not lead you where you will not be victorious. God leads us on the path that will yield the most growth and bring Him the glory.
3. You are never alone. Even in what appears to be your darkest hour, God is with you. The angels are ministering to you.

The enemy comes immediately to challenge who you are. All that you go through, the obstacles, the backbiting, the tears and the pain all were designed to challenge who you are. But God allowed it to show you whose you are. Satan only flees when the word is spoken. You cannot fight him alone, through your own might. You must use the word.

It is no coincidence that as soon as you accepted the call on your life that you were met with opposition. You see, Satan cannot stop God's plan, in fact, he does not even know he is a participant. But he tries to delay your arrival and delay your impact on the Earth. Procrastination, frustration, confusion, and the attack on your family and finances are all the devices he uses to distract and delay you. Don't give in. Don't give up. Stay focused, remember who you are. Seek him daily and in the time of temptation, the word will prevail.

**PRAYER:** *Father I thank you that your word says we are not ignorant of the enemy's devices. I bind distraction, fear, and procrastination right now in the name of Jesus. I cancel the attack of the enemy on my family and my finances. I speak life and rejuvenation and ask that you give me strength to continue in the plans you have for me. In Jesus' name, Amen.*

**Reflection and Reaction**

Regardless of what it looks or feels like, you are never alone.

God chose you and is well pleased. You are already victorious.

Repeat these statements daily:

I am chosen by God

I am pleasing in His sight

I am victorious

I am never alone

# 64

# Blind Faith

*Then Jesus said to them, "Follow Me and I will make you become fishers of men." They immediately left their nets and followed Him.*

*Mark 1:17-18*

Did they know what it meant to be "fishers of men"? Did they ask? We assume that because there is no mention of questioning perhaps they knew what they were agreeing to.

Did they know who Jesus was? Were they amongst the crowd at Jesus' baptism, therefore witnessing the Spirit descending upon him and the voice declaring Him the Son of God? Probably not!

What we do know is, they immediately left their nets…..their jobs, their comfort zone, their homes, their families and followed Him. What was it about their lives, at that very moment that they decided to leave it all behind?

"Immediate" requires quick decision and quick action. No time for the enemy to cast doubt and fear. No time for second guessing. No time to count the cost. No time for a second opinion. Sometimes you got to let your heart make the decisions and tell your mind to mind its business.

"Follow Me and I will make you become" is a powerful statement. When God asks us to do something, there is always a reward for your obedience. He knows the sacrifice you will make and the tribulations you will face as a result of your decision. One thing for sure, there is no becoming if you don't first follow Christ. Your way will never work, though it may appear so at first but without Christ it will soon crumble.

God is faithful. He is a man of His word. Remember what He promised you will become and hold tight to it. Trust His plan. "Become" is a process. Submit to the process. Be patient in the wait. Blind faith not only implies that one is unable to see the path ahead but more importantly it means that you are trusting the one who is leading.

**PRAYER:** *Dear God, thank you for your word being a lamp unto my feet. Help me to remember that your way is what is best for me and your process will yield the greatest reward. Teach me to trust you though your plan may not always be clear. I surrender to your will. I acknowledge you in all my ways. As I submit to the process, I thank you for increased clarity to accomplish the purpose that you have given. In Jesus' name, Amen.*

## Reflection and Reaction

Without faith it is impossible to please God.

Do you have the faith to: leave your comfort zone, make an immediate decision to eliminate doubt, and become someone new?

Know that your faith will be tested, but know also that you have the victory.

# 65

# One With Authority

*And they were astonished at His teaching, for He taught them as one having authority and not as the scribes.*

*Mark 1:22*

Jesus spoke with authority, given to Him by God, as someone who knows versus the scribes who only wrote what they heard from others accounts. When you know who you are, you have the authority or power to command your atmosphere. You and God become one in partnership to impart to others. You become wise beyond personal knowledge. You become God in the Earth. Basically the anointing takes over.

We have to understand that our gifts and talents are not just for us. They were not given to us for personal gain, such as money or material possession. Rather your gifts are for the kingdom, that God's people will be blessed, healed, delivered, set-free, and for His glory. As long as you remain selfish, you will remain in darkness and your gift will be worthless.

God will not be mocked. His word will not return to Him void. This does not mean that Christians are to only use their gifts in the church. In fact, as Christians, we are instructed to go beyond the church walls. But what it means is that God's word will accomplish what He intended it to do. If your gift does not lead or draw others to Christ, if it does not glorify or reverence God, it is not being used appropriately.

Do not be deceived, God's gifts come without repentance. Satan tries to imitate God. Therefore don't get weary in well-doing because you see others, unbelievers, being prosperous. In due season they will reap what they sow. Remember God has called you! God has spoken to you! Work out your own salvation with trembling and fear. Don't get frustrated in the lack of support. Be bold, be courageous, you have the authority. Do what He told you to do, exactly how He told you to do it, and watch God perform. He will draw the right people to you.

**PRAYER:** *Dear Heavenly Father, thank you for the authority you have given me to do your will. Help me to remain humble and remember it is about you and leading others to salvation. Where I am weary and weak, thank you for your strength. When I am frustrated, thank you for your peace. Teach me how to boldly accomplish the task set before me. In Jesus' name, Amen.*

## Reflection and Reaction

The key to walking in authority is belief!

Do you believe that God chose you?

Do you believe you have what it takes?

Do you believe that you are equipped with everything you need?

______________________________________________

______________________________________________

______________________________________________

______________________________________________

______________________________________________

______________________________________________

______________________________________________

______________________________________________

______________________________________________

______________________________________________

______________________________________________

______________________________________________

______________________________________________

______________________________________________

# 66

# Worth Talking About

*And when the unclean spirit had convulsed him and cried out with a loud voice, he came out of him. Then they were all amazed, so that they questioned among themselves saying, "What is this? What new doctrine is this? For with authority He commands even the unclean spirits and they obey Him. And immediately His fame spread throughout all the region around Galilee.*

*Mark 1: 26-28*

In these verses we again see Jesus cast out an unclean spirit. But notice a few things:

1. The enemy is not quiet. An unclean spirit sneaks in quietly but fights on the way out! This is why when people want to change, the flesh acts out and speaks louder. The people are not weak, they just don't know what to do about that annoying voice.
2. They were amazed. People are amazed by what they can't do themselves. What is different about you? Are you blending in or are you showing others a different way, approach, or lifestyle. This is why the word tells us to come from among them. You can't draw others to Christ if you are acting and living like the very ones you are trying to save.
3. His fame spread. Your actions speak for you. If you are not spreading, it is because you are not doing anything worth talking about. Jesus lived in a time without automobiles, cell phones, television, and social media. Yet His fame spread!

Miracles followed Jesus. He did not go looking for them. He did not sit and wait for them to come to Him either. As He walked …. As you go … God will work through you. Be ye holy, for I am holy. In a world where holiness seems unpopular, God is elevating those who keep His word and live a righteous lifestyle. The world is looking for God. They are looking for hope. Are there any righteous among you says the Lord? Are there any willing to do my will says God. Holiness is still the way.

God has not forgotten. Remember the story of Job. Satan was seeking to and fro. God asked him "have you considered my servant Job?" Job was attacked because God was bragging on Him. Job was attacked because he was considered righteous in the land. Yes he lost a lot, but he received double for his trouble AND he was an example to his friends of the faithfulness of God. Keep living right. It will pay off. In due season you shall reap, if you faint not. Someone is always watching. Good news travels fast. Soon you will be worth talking about. Soon your fame, His glory, will spread. Stay in the word, stay in his presence. Allow God to do, speak, and work through you. Surrender daily! Sacrifice daily! Relinquish control daily!

**PRAYER:** *Dear Heavenly Father, Help me to not get frustrated in well doing. Your word says one plants, another waters but it is you who gets the increase. I surrender to you today. Help me to be an excellent representation of your love and kindness on today. Help me to not be concerned about my own popularity but to remember that only what I do for you counts. As I relinquish control on today, help me to remember that you know what's best for me and have an expected end in mind. In Jesus' name, Amen.*

**<u>Reflection and Reaction</u>**

Are you worth talking about?

Your idea, gift, purpose, etc. may seem identical to someone else's but what is unique about you? What do you do differently?

Don't envy others, discover your own specialty. The people will be drawn to that which you do differently.

________________________________________

________________________________________

________________________________________

________________________________________

# 67

# Discernment Is Crucial

*At evening, when the sun had set, they brought to Him all who were sick and those who were demon possessed. And the whole city was gathered together at the door. Then He healed many who were sick with various diseases, and case out many demons; and He did not allow the demons to speak, because they knew Him.*

*Mark 1: 31-34*

*Now a leper came to Him, imploring Him, kneeling down to Him and saying to Him, "If you are willing, You can make me clean." The Jesus, moved with compassion, stretched out His hand and touched him, and said to him, "I am willing; be cleansed." As soon as He had spoken, immediately the leprosy left him, and he was cleansed. And He strictly warned him and sent him away at once, and said to him, "See that you say nothing to anyone, but go your way, show yourself to the priest, and offer for your cleansing those things which Moses commanded, as a testimony to them." However he went out and began to proclaim it freely, and to spread the matter, so that Jesus could no longer openly enter the city, but was outside in deserted places; and they came to Him from every direction.*

*Mark 1: 40-45*

Have you ever wondered why Jesus asked people not to tell others how He healed them? The object was to get as many people saved as possible, wasn't it? As many times as I have read these passages, I never paid attention or never questioned why. He had kingdom discernment, and knew it was not the appropriate time. He controlled the rising of his fame. Again we learn multiple lessons in leadership and success:

1. In advertisement, your spokesperson matters. The demons were not the right spokesperson. The haters or spectators where already questioning Jesus' authority. If a demon praised him, the people would think His power came from Satan and not God. Be sure that the right people, with the right character are singing your praises. Association can affect your ministry and/or business depending on the reputation of the person. This is true in the natural as well. An athlete can get many endorsements as long as he is an upstanding citizen, but when his actions depict that of immoral or illegal behavior, those endorsements are pulled quickly. Why, because that company does not want their business associated with questionable behavior.
2. Timing is everything. Though Jesus was moved by compassion to heal the leper, he too was warned to not express his gratitude openly. We quickly see why. The people began to come to him without allowing him to enter the cities, without allowing him to go to the people who needed him most. They began to be only interested in one aspect of who He was. They were buying the product without hearing the message. The healing was only temporary, but the message gave them eternal life.

The natural leader in us want to be recognized for our gifts. We want the people to love us and follow us. We want notoriety, monetary gain, and financial success. We want our business, our ministry, etc. to blow up overnight. However discernment is key. We must know when the appointed time has come. As visionaries we are often mesmerized by "all of a sudden" rises to fame or status. But we must remember that anything that happens overnight or all of a sudden, can also be lost all of a sudden. Allow God to perfect your gift and to develop and prepare you for His platform.

How you start is important. Yes it may take longer, but it will also last longer and be more appreciated. Don't allow someone else's attachment for selfish gain cause you to jump out of season. Don't allow your gifts to be exploited to someone else's agenda. Don't allow your gifts to be misused and thus become a detriment to the kingdom. Don't despise the preparation phase. God's timing is perfect. Be patient, stay prayerful, keep reading and meditating, on His word. At the appointed time, right on time, you will spring forth.

**PRAYER:** *Dear Lord, thank you for choosing me as your servant. Help me to remember that you have plans for me of prosperity to give me hope and a future. Thank you for reminding me that you are always mindful of me. Thank you for perfecting that which concerneth me. Help me to stay on track and not attempt to jump before my time. Thank you for kingdom discernment to discern those things that are not of you and people who have their own agenda or ulterior motives. Your word says my gift will make room for me and bring me before great men. In Jesus' name, Amen.*

## Reflection and Reaction

Timing and character are key components of discernment.

Are you rushing up the ladder or towards fame?

Are you seeking popularity regardless of who helps or who speaks for you?

Be patient and allow God control.

All publicity is not good publicity. Test the character of the spokesperson.

# 68

# The Cost of Fame

*But immediately, when Jesus perceived in His spirit that they reasoned this within themselves, He said to them "Why do you reason about these things in your hearts? Which is easier to say to the paralytic, 'Your sins are forgiven you' or to say 'Arise, take up your bed and walk?' But that you may know that the Son of Man has power on earth to forgive sins."*

*Mark 2: 8-10*

Just as Jesus' fame spread and the multitude followed Him everywhere He went, so did His haters! His ministry had just begun, yet there were people following Him, not for healing, not for salvation, not for deliverance, but to question everything He was doing. Up to this point, though they questioned Him, they were not as bothered with His display of miraculous works as with this one. They were cool with the laying on of hands and healing, but how dare He proclaim to give forgiveness of sins. Forgiveness was a power only God could give…or so they thought.

There are two important revelations we can take from this passage:

1. Know who you are. People will try to put you a box or may not understand the fullness of your gift. The people followed the gift, they were astonished by the miracles, and they did not know who He was! Stay focused, you must know your assignment.
2. Haters also have a role. There is no such thing as bad publicity as long as you continue to do what's right. Jesus did not defend himself, He questioned their understanding.

On the road to success, or shall I say, on the journey to fulfill your purpose, you must accept the bitter with the sweet. Amongst the praises will also be those who seek to destroy you. Not because of jealousy or hatred but because the work of the Lord in you and through you. Your presence will challenge their very existence. Greatness will either inspire greatness or expose weakness. When weakness is challenged it will fight to appear strong.

Jesus is our example of how to behave under pressure. First, don't stop. Continue in the work of the Lord. Continue in the plans He has given you. Secondly remain humble. It is not the time to boast or brag on your previous victories. Nor is it the time to defend your honor or your works. Lastly have confidence in what God called you to do. Don't take it personal. It is not you they are rejecting.

**PRAYER:** *Dear Lord, I thank you for your Son Jesus being an example of how to walk in confidence to fulfill your purpose. Help me to remember that it is not about me. Help me to remember that the battle is not mine but yours. Help me to remember to pray and meditate daily that I may be strengthened in your word. In Jesus' name, Amen.*

## Reflection and Reaction

The bible teaches us to consider the costs.

Do you want success but complain about the hard work?

Do you want promotion or more money but complain about the increase in responsibility?

Do you want your own business but complain about workers or customer dissatisfaction?

Learn to take the good with the bad while keeping your character and integrity intact.

________________________________________

________________________________________

________________________________________

________________________________________

________________________________________

________________________________________

________________________________________

# 69

# A House Divided Cannot Stand

*And if a house is divided against itself, that house cannot stand. And if Satan has risen up against himself, and is divided, he cannot stand, but has and end. No one can enter a strong man's house and plunder his goods, unless he first binds the strong man. And then he will plunder his house.*

*Mark 3: 25-27*

The journey towards purpose must be one of intent. Once you discover what God created you to do, you must make a conscious and heartfelt decision to see it through. Remember purpose is a life mission. It is not the completion of one goal or the fulfillment of a dream. It is a decision to allow God to be Lord over your life and lead you toward "life more abundantly." It is a journey of growth, maturity, strategic choices and sacrifices.

It will not be easy. Don't assume that you will be skipping along, smelling roses and sipping tea. Times will get rough. People will turn their backs on you. There will be days or even years where you will feel alone. It will be stretching. But know that it will be worth it.

A house divided cannot stand. Who you hang around, what you do, and what you say must align with your purpose. If any of those contradict, you must walk away or you are setting yourself up for failure. Choose people who support and encourage your dreams to spend time with. Remove people who remind you of your past and feed negativity in your life. Choose activities that feed your spirit man and align with the new you and how you want to be remembered. Eliminate wasteful activities.

A house divided cannot stand. Examine yourself daily. Change your thoughts and the words you speak towards yourself. Speak words of encouragement to yourself. Eliminate words of negative connotation. The bible teaches us that our words are spirit and life. Don't allow anyone including yourself to kill your dreams or your spirit. Spend time with God, read the word, pray and meditate daily. The word will keep you grounded, it will keep you encouraged, it will give you direction and specific instructions, and it will keep you on track.

**PRAYER:** *Dear Heavenly Father, Thank you for showing me that my life is important. Thank you for discernment and teaching me how to choose people, things, and activities that align with my purpose and the plan you have for my life. Thank you for divine connections and thank you for giving me the strength and faith to remove all people, things, and distractions that keep me away from my goals or attempt to get me off track. As I grow and mature in you, I thank you for enlarging my territory and helping me to remember that you are with me always. In Jesus' name, Amen.*

## Reflection and Reaction

Purpose must be protected!

Do you hang with people who contradict the character and lifestyle that God wants you to portray?

Do you allow yourself or others to speak against your gifts or dreams?

What you hear and what you do, including who you hear it from and do it with, affect your thoughts and actions.

Make an effort to eliminate all negativity by any means necessary.

________________________________________________

________________________________________________

________________________________________________

________________________________________________

________________________________________________

________________________________________________

________________________________________________

________________________________________________

# 70

# Birds of a Feather Flock Together

*For whoever does the will of God is My brother and My sister and mother*

*Mark 3:35*

I know I have mentioned it before but this is a crucial step in accepting and walking in purpose. Surround yourself with those who are seeking and doing the will of God. Many fall short or give up at this stage. Honestly it is understandable. No one wants to be alone, especially when you feel you are becoming a better person and on the road to doing great things. Everyone, your family, your friends, should be happy for you! Wrong.

Attempting to hold on to people can actually be more of a hindrance and also quite stressful. You end up spending more time questioning your lack of support and encouragement than actually completing goals and moving forward. I remember when I finished my first book. I was so excited. People said they were excited too but when the book came out, how quickly tables turned. When I needed people to buy the book, they turned their backs. When I needed support at events, no one showed. When I needed help with marketing, no one had time. When I wanted feedback and reviews, no one actually read the book to give a review. I had to realize that lip service was all the support some could give. I also learned that I was seeking validation from others.

Another key step in pursuing purpose, is examining your motives. Are you wanting exaltation from others or God? Is praise from others the source of your motivation? Do you need a physical pat on the back as confirmation that you made the right decision? I had to realize it was my dream, not theirs. Be grateful for what they can give and don't worry about what they can't. God will bring the right people who need your service, business or gift. Obedience is key. God requires us to do what he told us to do, the results are up to Him.

Who you associate with can actually lead to stagnation. Find friends, groups, etc. that feed your passion. Find friends, groups, etc. that are go-getters and determined to make their dreams come true. Surround yourself with like-minded people. Even if they can't physically fund your dreams, they can teach you what they have learned along the way. Knowledge and time is more valuable than money. People who have no dreams, stopped dreaming or are afraid to go after their dreams do not understand the plight of a visionary. If you want your own business, join a group of entrepreneurs or networking group. Invest in you. You don't have to beg for support if you surround yourself with the right people. Remember people will either influence you or you will influence them; generally the majority wins. If you are the smartest one, the only one wanting a better life, or the one everyone comes to for help, find a different group. Iron sharpens iron.

**PRAYER:** *Dear Heavenly Father, Thank you for being my strength. Thank you for your Holy Spirit being my guide as I walk in faith towards your will for my life. Help me to choose those people who are beneficial to me and will help me fulfill my purpose. Help me to remove those who are hindrances to my growth and I thank you now for peace in making those decisions. Also help me to be patient as your perfect will is revealed in my life. In Jesus' name, Amen.*

**Reflection and Reaction**

Association is key to purpose. It can make or break you.

Assess the people in your life:

1. Who challenges you? (Initiates new ideas)
2. Who encourages you? (Prevents you from giving up)
3. Who celebrates you? (genuinely happy for you)

If you don't have these types in your circle, let them go and go find those who do.

# 71

# Hear and Obey

*If anyone has ears to hear, let him hear. Then He said to them, "Take heed to what you hear. With the same measure you use, it will be measured to you; and to you who hear, more will be given. For whoever has, to him more will be given, but whoever does not have, even what he has will be taken away from him."*

*Mark 4: 23-25*

Have you ever noticed how many times "let him who has ears, let him hear" or a similar phrase is mentioned in the book of Mark and wondered why? One morning while reading chapter 4 in the book of Mark, the Holy Spirit urged me to look up the Greek meaning for "hear." Hear is derived from the Greek word "shema" and is defined as listening, taking heed, and responding with action to what one has heard. It is synonymous with obey – to hear – is to do and obey. Therefore that brief text can be translated as "You have heard my teachings, now take it to heart and obey it!"

Obedience is key when it comes to matters of heaven. Obedience moves God. It builds God's confidence in you. It builds your strength and character. The more you do what He tells you, the more He will give you. Likewise the opposite, those who are disobedient (refuse to follow instructions), even what he has (gifts and talents) will be taken away.

Well doing produces more fruit. The more you hear and obey, more will be given. Which again is the importance of staying in God's presence, maintaining a close relationship with Him and studying His word. Faith comes by hearing and hearing by the word of God (Romans 10:17). Faith is exercised and strengthened through obedience.

We are also warned to be careful of how we use what we hear. As we will be held accountable. Teachers are responsible for ensuring the truth is taught, not their truth but God's truth. Using a platform of leadership and influence with conniving and evil intentions toward others will lead followers astray and invoke the wrath of God.

The magnitude of success is not measured by the greatness of the gift or talent or material possessions. But rather by the ability and the quickness of the person to yield to God's command. Kingdom mentality and kingdom instruction yield the keys to the kingdom. If you listen to God, the reward is from heaven and is way bigger than you can imagine. Likewise, worldly mentality and worldly instruction yield worldly rewards. It is only for a season and can die with you. Are you building a legacy to pass on to your children's children or just trying to make life more comfortable for you?

**PRAYER:** *Heavenly Father, thank you for your word on today. Forgive me for not heeding your instructions. Help me to focus on your will and how my gifts and talent will benefit the kingdom. Open my spiritual hears that I may heed your voice and quicken my steps that I may obey your commands. I bind fear now in the name of Jesus that causes me to procrastinate and ask that you replace it with confidence and trust that you know the plans you have for me. In Jesus' name, Amen.*

## Reflection and Reaction

We must learn to hear and obey.

What did you hear the Lord say?

What actions are you taking to obey what you hear?

We cannot continue to seek a word from the Lord, yet refuse to take action when it is given.

Until you do what He said the first time, He will not give you the next set of instructions.

_______________________________________________

_______________________________________________

_______________________________________________

_______________________________________________

_______________________________________________

# 72

# I Am God's Seed

*And He said, "The kingdom of God is as if a man should scatter seed on the ground, and should sleep by night and rise by day, and the seed should sprout and grow, he himself does not know how. For the earth yields crops by itself: first the blade, then the head, after that the full grain in head. But when the grain ripens, immediately he puts in the sickle, because the harvest has come."*

*Mark 4: 26-29*

We are the Earth. God's seed is already in us. The seed will sprout and grow but we do not know when we are ripened and ready to be used. Nor should we be concerned. God plants, waters and will receive the increase. We must trust that what He has planted he will also water and ensure its growth. We must trust that our season of ripening, producing fruit, will come at His appointed time.

We must not worry with timing. Timing is the most difficult concept in the mind of believers. God does not live in time though He placed us in time. The good news is, time will not run out before His will is done. IF we continue to keep His commands. We must remember regardless of what it looks like, regardless of how much time has passed, His word will accomplish what it set out to do. This is where faith comes in. During the watering, faith is tested multiple times. This is also why the journey is so important. He adds to our faith along the way and the lessons learned will equip you for the assignments He has before you. Don't give up, the harvest is coming.

We also must not worry with knowing. Fear of the unknown is debilitating. It is not necessary to know or be forewarned when the harvest has come or is approaching. What is important to remember is that it will all work out for our good. God's way, the journey, is not always sunshine and blue skies. The rain is also necessary. Sometimes, most times, when it rains it pours. But the word reminds us in Psalm 119:71, "It is good for me that I have been afflicted; that I might learn thy statutes." There is purpose in the pain. Rather than ask "why me?" ask "what wisdom should I gain from this experience." This line of questioning may not make the pain go away but it will ensure it is worth it. Don't give up, God promised beauty for ashes.

**PRAYER:** *Dear Lord, God of heaven and earth, thank you for the seed you have placed in me. Help me to endure growth as a good soldier. Help me to remember that you will perfect that which concerns me. Help me to remember that your word will not return to you void and will accomplish what you command. Thank you for increased wisdom and understanding of the trials you have placed in my path. As I walk with you, help me to rest in your presence. In Jesus' name, Amen.*

## Reflection and Reaction

Does timing and fear of what lies ahead prevent you from doing what God called you to do?

Perhaps delusional expectations are preventing you to see when your harvest has come.

The time is now. Trust you are right where you are supposed to be. Rather than watching the clock, watch God!

# 73

# Don't Despise Small Beginnings

*Then He said, "To what shall we liken the kingdom of God? Or with what parable shall we picture it? It is like a mustard seed which, when it is sown on the ground, is smaller than all the seeds on earth; but when it is sown, it grows up and becomes greater than all herbs and shoots out large branches so that the birds of the air may rest under its shade."*

*Mark 4: 30-32*

The things and the mind of God are sometimes hard to fathom, especially to a hardened heart. But if we can grasp the concept of kingdom mentality, that the kingdom of God is IN us, we can begin to understand the power that we possess. God created us to succeed. We are His namesake.

Don't despise small beginnings. You may feel insignificant now but God is growing you up. As you increase in God and learn to trust without doubting, you will be greater than you even imagine. As you grow, your gifts will magnify so that others will take refuge under your branches. Your desire to be significant, important, or great in your own eyes, cannot overshadow the desire to be in God's will.

God is not logical. He does not respond to logical thinking. Allow Him to open your eyes of understanding that you may be enlightened of the heart of God. Growing pains are necessary to remove pride and personal ambition. Don't get me wrong, it is not erroneous to desire success and material possession, but it is wrong to place such desires in high priority over purpose.

Don't despise small beginnings. Why are you in such a rush? Be anxious for nothing. The seed does not rush the sower. A farmer does not watch the seed. He just knows that if He waters and tills the land, it will produce fruit. The word reminds us that there is a time for everything under the sun, a time for planting and a time for harvest, a time for reaping and a time for sowing. Enjoy this time. Cultivate your gift. Learn all you can. Find a role-model. Join a professional organization or group. How you wait determines how long you wait. Ask God for direction and get busy.

**PRAYER:** *Dear Lord, thank you for the seed of success that is within me. Thank you for teaching me how to be patient and wait on you. As I wait I ask that you give me direction on how to be a good steward over my gift and manage my time wisely. I thank you for your word that says though the vision may tarry, wait for it because it will surely come. Thank you for your faithfulness and kindness towards me. In Jesus' name, Amen.*

## Reflection and Reaction

Many times we overlook the journey chasing the destination.

Are you overlooking the small victories looking for a miracle?

Are you unable to see the beauty of the forest staring at the height of the trees?

Every small step gets you closer to the bigger goal. Take joy in and be grateful for the small steps.

# 74

# No Need to Fear, Jesus is Here

*But He said to them, "Why are you so fearful? How is it that you have no faith?"*

*Mark 4:40*

How can you have no faith when Jesus is with you? When you have witnessed His hand at work in your life? Because you have yet to discover who Jesus is! You do not understand and have yet to grasp, the power in His name. You are God in the earth. The power of heaven is living inside YOU, working in YOU!

No need to fear, Jesus is here! When you know Jesus is with you, your super powers are activated.

You can fly.

You can speak to mountains.

You can tread on serpents.

You can cast out demons.

You can call those things that be not as though they were.

You are victorious.

You are more than a conqueror.

You are more than enough.

You can do all things, through Christ who strengthens you.

You can break down walls.

You can walk through rivers on dry land.

You can walk on water.

You can heal the sick, make the lame walk and the blind to see.

Why? Because greater things you will do! (John 14:12). The myth is that fear should not exist in the mind and actions of believers. Fear is not of God, but even God recognized its existence. Do not fear is mentioned 365 times in the bible! We have to learn what to do when it peaks its ugly head. The problem, according to any school teacher or psychologist, is that fear can be a necessary component in times of trouble. It can alert you when something is not right. But it can also give a false sense of danger when one is venturing outside of his/her comfort zone. Therefore to properly handle fear, we must immediately access the situation. Am I in danger or potential danger? Or am I leery of the unknown? Remember there is no failure in God. He can do everything but fail. Failure only exists when we refuse to accept the lesson in things not turning out the way we hoped. God is strategic, his plan encompasses the good and the not so good. The more you trust Him, the more fear will subside.

**PRAYER:** *Dear Lord, Thank you for your supernatural strength living in me. Thank you for showing me that fear is not of you. I thank you that the same power that you have, I have. Help me to walk in victory. Help me to quickly turn to you when fear arises. Help me to utilize fear as motivation rather than allowing it to cause me to doubt your will for my life. As I trust you, help me to accomplish my assignments in spite of fear. In Jesus' name, Amen.*

## Reflection and Reaction

What are you afraid of?

Have you allowed fear to stagnate your wants and dreams?

Assess your fears and give it over to God.

Quick action prevents fear from taking root.

____________________________________________

____________________________________________

____________________________________________

# 75

# The Key to Success is in Your Testimony

*And when He got into the boat, he who had been demon-possessed begged Him that he might be with Him. However, Jesus did not permit him, but said to him, "Go home to your friends, and tell them what great things the Lord has done for you, and how He has had compassion on you." And he departed and began to proclaim in Decapolis all that Jesus had done for him, and all marveled.*

*Mark 5: 18-20*

Many times people wonder what their purpose is, what they were created to do, and often bow their heads down in shame and frustration when posed the question from others. Until purpose is discovered, it is the scariest thing that people can imagine. Not because of the impossibility of being able to fulfill it but because of the implication that they have wasted time doing the wrong thing. No one likes to waste time, at least not on non-pleasurable activities. But I would like to offer you another perspective.

Discovering your purpose is a lifelong activity. In reality, the excitement, the motivation, the fuel of happiness is in discovering the gift, or natural ability, that God will use to give you purpose. It's the gift that keeps on giving. It's the gift that's already in you. It's your go to in times of stress. It's that thing that makes you angry when it is abused. It's that thing that makes you smile when it is celebrated. It's that thing that makes you cry when it is misunderstood. You don't have to think about it. You don't have to try hard. It's just in you. Most people put it to the side and view it as a hobby.

The key to success, the key to utilizing your gift successfully, is in your testimony. It's so simple, yet so complicated. God does not ask for what we do not have or what we have not done. Tap into the why. I never saw writing as a gift. I began writing as a child because I didn't have anyone to talk to. I started writing in my journal about my day. Then I began to be bullied at school and started writing about that. Writing became a way for me to release the pain without shame and embarrassment. As I ventured into middle and high school, I stopped writing but began to read more. I would escape from my problems in the pages of my favorite books. Then about 10 years ago, when I rededicated my life to Christ, I started taking notes in church, reading my bible and praying. The voice of the Lord came to me so quickly. I was excited, yet it felt strange, so I began to write down what I heard. Then I started asking questions and watched Him answer them in the pages of my notebook. One question "Why am I still single?" and he provided me with a whole book as the answer. Now I write to provide others with the same healing and encouragement He gave me.

Your purpose, your gift, is in your testimony. What has God done for you? How has He brought you out? The compassion He showed you, you must show others. Look back over your life. Pay attention to what has worked rather than your mistakes or what you think you missed. Purpose is found in either our passion or our pain. Most times it's a combination of both, because pain leads us to compassion towards the afflicted. There is no waste in God. All things work together for our good. All that you have done and have been through God has need of.

**PRAYER:** *Dear Heavenly Father, I come to you today seeking your guidance in discovering my gifts and the purpose you created for me to use those gifts. You are a marvelous and all-knowing God who created me with a purpose and a plan. I thank you now for opening my spiritual eyes that I may see the greatness of discovering who I am in you. In Jesus' name, Amen.*

## Reflection and Reaction

To discover you purpose ask yourself three questions:

1. What's my passion? What makes you laugh, cry, or angry? What cause do you tend to support? **This is your why**

2. What pain am I hiding? What are you past hurts? What did you survive or what struggle did you overcome? **This is your audience or your who**
3. What do I know (knowledge/education, experiences and hobbies)? **These are your gifts or your how**

# 76

# They Can't See You

*But Jesus said to them, "A prophet is not without honor except in his own country, among his own relatives, and in his own house."*

*Mark 6: 4*

Who can deny the power of Jesus? His folks did! When I read this chapter in Mark I was so frustrated at the folks at Nazareth. They watched him perform miracles, healing the blind, casting out demons, and causing the lame to walk. Yet they called him "the carpenter, son of Mary, and brother of James, Joses, Judas, and Simon!" (Vs 3) The nerve of them. Then I wondered why did God even allow it to be written in the bible? Why are any of the bad things written about Jesus in the bible for that matter? That we may know He understands ALL that we go through and to be an example of what to do when we go through it.

Familiarity breeds contempt and offense. Those around you can't see who you are or appreciate your gift because they are viewing you through their own eyes, their own abilities, their own failures, their own mistakes, their own willingness or lack thereof. How is it that you, being from the same family, same household, same city, same educational opportunities, and same experiences can be so different? What makes you so special? How dare you shine light on their inadequacies by being great, desiring more, AND telling everybody about it! Because of who they are not, they can't see you for who you are.

We have all heard the saying "Misery loves company," well the opposite is also true. Happiness loves company too! So what do you do? Run, Forest, Run! Jesus did not stay there, He did not try to explain himself. He helped who He could and left. You do not have to stay where you are not appreciated. You do not have to remain loyal to a relationship that is not equally yoked. They will stifle you while you are there and talk about you when you are gone. Choose you. Choose God's plan for your life. Forsake all others and follow Him. What are you willing to sacrifice?

**PRAYER:** *Dear Lord of heaven and earth, I thank you for your glory being revealed in my life. I thank you for revelation in your word. I thank you for giving me the strength to walk away from anything and/or person that is a hindrance or is against the plan you have for my life. I thank you for divinely connecting me to others who will celebrate me, appreciate my gifts, and help move me towards your plan. In Jesus' name, Amen.*

## Reflection and Reaction

Are you still trying to hold on to the past or people familiar to your past? Are you struggling to convince others you have changed? Are you struggling to convince others to support and celebrate your purpose and gifts?

Purpose releases you from false loyalty!

You do not have to beg for support.

You do not have to prove your worth.

You do not have to stay.

The sooner you walk away, the sooner God can surround you with those who do!

________________________________________________________

________________________________________________________

________________________________________________________

________________________________________________________

________________________________________________________

________________________________________________________

________________________________________________________

________________________________________________________

________________________________________________________

# 77

# What You Have is Enough

*But He answered and said to them, "You give them something to eat." And they said to Him, "Shall we go and buy two hundred denarii worth of bread and give them something to eat?" But He said to them, "How many loaves do you have? Go and see." And when they found out they said, "Five, and two fish." Then He commanded them to make them all sit down in groups on the green grass. So they sat down in ranks, in hundreds and in fifties. And when He had taken the five loaves and the two fish, He looked up to heaven, blessed and broke the loaves, and gave them to His disciples to set before them; and the two fish He divided among them all. So they all ate and were filled. And they took up twelve baskets full of fragments and of the fish. Now those who had eaten the loaves were about five thousand men.*

*Mark 6: 37-44*

Many times we feel like we need something extra: more money, more time, another job, a spouse, a better car; more than we have, to do what God asked us to do. But all God wants is your obedience. There are several points in this passage that we need to acknowledge as we journey towards purpose.

First, you are expected to give the people something. Your gift (what you have) is the solution to someone's problem. In verse 37, Jesus commanded the disciples "you give them something to eat." In the verses before the disciples noticed it was getting late and the followers needed food. But they suggested Jesus send them away to fend for themselves. Funny how we can notice a problem, yet feel it ain't got nothing to do with us or it is not our issue to solve. But that which is common for you is needed by others.

Secondly, everything you need is in you. Assess what you have. God does not ask us to do what we are not capable of doing. The key is we need His help and we must acknowledge Him to accomplish it. What you think you need or what you assume you lack is only a hindrance. It is what the devil uses to fuel procrastination. Take inventory and place what you have in God's hands.

Third, what you have is more than enough. Obedience moves God. Allow Him to multiply what you have. He will make it stretch. He will ensure the people are fed. Many times we are attempting to do it all in our strength but it is the power of God propelling us that gives us our true strength.

Lastly, you don't have to be perfect. You don't have to have it all together. The gift does not have to be perfect before you begin. Verse 42 states "so they all ate and were filled." Your gift will feed you and others. Don't worry about eating first, you can eat with the people. Let God be glorified, all He requires is that you be willing and obedient.

Don't be overwhelmed by what you don't have or what you can't do. God wants who you are and what you got. He wants to use what you have. The problem is you don't think you have anything. But God say's you are more than enough. Look to heaven and watch Him multiply. Do what you can, don't be stressed out over what you can't.

**PRAYER:** *Heavenly Father I thank you for the plan you have for my life. I thank you for the gifts and talents you have placed in me. Help me to be obedient to your instructions without fear. Help me to acknowledge you in all my ways. Help me to remember that what you have called me to do, you have also equipped me to do. I thank you for your Holy Spirit in me that not only leads and guides me into all truth but also gives me the power to complete the tasks you have set before me. In Jesus' name, Amen.*

## Reflection and Reaction

God knew what you had when He called you, when He formed you in the womb!

God knows it, but you need time to discover it.

Take inventory of what you have.

Rather than complain about what is missing, be grateful for what is there and ask God to multiply it.

__________________________________________________

__________________________________________________

__________________________________________________

__________________________________________________

# 78

# Revelation Proceeds Understanding

*Then He saw them straining at rowing, for the wind was against them. Now about the fourth watch of the night, He came to them, walking on the sea and would have passed them by. And when they saw Him walking on the sea, they supposed it was a ghost, and cried out; for they all saw Him and were troubled. But immediately He talked with them and said to them, "Be of good cheer! It is I, do not be afraid." Then He went up into the boat to them and the wind ceased. And they were greatly amazed in themselves beyond measure and marveled. For they had not understood about the loaves because their heart was hardened.*

*Mark 6: 48-52*

One of the biggest myths of Christians and Christianity is perfection. Christians don't have it all together. Perfection is not a prerequisite to be a disciple. The miracles were as much for His disciples as they were for the people. They still did not understand who Jesus was. Though they walked with Him, they did not know Him. They had no revelation of who He was. Fear hardens our heart and prevents our spiritual awakening.

We can be in such a hurry to do the work and get the blessings of God, that we overlook the process and transformation that must take place. Before God can use you, you must bear witness of who He is and His power. You cannot tell, teach, or write etc. about what you do not know. Our reach is limited, not by our resources but by the depth of our testimony. The more you learn the more you have to teach. The more you experience, the more you have to tell.

Be patient. As you increase in your knowledge of God, God will enlarge your territory. The desire to know Him and please Him must be stronger than the desire for fame, material gain, wealth, etc. There is purpose in your pain; a lesson in every experience. Use this time, while you wait, to take inventory of all that God has done and His character He has revealed. It can be scary getting to know someone new, even if that someone new is God, rather than fear the unknown, embrace the revelation.

Revelation proceeds understanding. Let go of the false sense of what you think you know. Open your heart to learning. Struggle and waiting do not always equate to disobedience. Ask God to reveal the lesson He wants you to learn. Be of good cheer and allow the Lord to amaze and marvel you!

**PRAYER:** *Dear Lord thank you for taking the time and attention to reveal yourself to me. I embrace getting to know you and basking in your presence. I let go of what I thought I knew or what was taught to me incorrectly and welcome a new awakening in you. As you open the eyes of my understanding, help me to be patient and enjoy the journey. I thank you that the work you begun in me, you shall see it through till completion. In Jesus' name, Amen.*

## Reflection and Reaction

Always remain teachable.

The lessons are more important than the journey.

Do you know God for yourself? Through your trials, what character traits has He revealed of Himself?

# 79

# Defilement Comes from Within

*There is nothing that enters a man from outside which can defile him; but the things which come out of him, those are the things that defile a man.*

*Mark 7: 15*

*So He said to them, "Are you thus without understanding also? Do you not perceive that whatever enters a man from outside cannot defile him, because it does not enter his heart but his stomach, and is eliminated, thus purifying all foods?"*

*Mark 7: 18-19*

If you are like me, you should have let out a loud "Ouch!" when reading this verse. I know Jesus is speaking of sin and the desire to commit sin comes from within. But from a dream and purpose perspective, I believe He was saying "No excuses. You have the power."

No excuses for you to not do what He has called you to do. Outside influences have no relevance. It does not matter what happened in the past: who hurt you, who left, who stayed, abuse, trauma, etc. None of it can erase the call God has on your life. Sure they caused a delay and/or attempted to make you give up. God instilled a purpose within you at creation. Jeremiah 1:5 proclaims "before He formed you in the womb, He knew you." That desire to be and to do, regardless of how much dirt was shoveled on top of you, the seed still remains. As long as you live, there will be an inner voice, the voice of the creator, nudging you, urging you, reminding you that you were meant to do more.

You have the power within. The power of life and death is in the tongue. What you say, the words you speak will either push you forward or push you down. You can decide today, and everyday thereafter, which direction you want to go. If you continue to tell yourself you're lazy, your gift is not important, you can't do it, you are no better that him or her, you don't have the strength, you are tired, you are stressed, you don't have enough money, you don't have enough support, etc.….then guess what you're right. Negative words produce negative behavior. On the flip side, positive words, produce positive behavior. When you began the day with "I Am," the angels stand at attention awaiting your command, and take flight at its release to accomplish it. Perhaps you may not feel it immediately. But if you keep repeating it, eventually you will take steps to make it a reality.

Defilement comes from within. Don't be your own worst enemy. Don't help the devil accomplish his plan to hinder who you become. Don't stand in your own way. Do take one day at a time. Do begin each day with prayer. Do allow yourself time to grow. Practice patience with yourself. You don't want to be in the presence of negativity and drama from others, therefore don't allow thoughts of inadequacy and fear hinder the many blessings and success that God has in store.

**PRAYER:** *Dear Heavenly Father, forgive me for the thoughts and actions, that were not of you and that I allowed to keep me from pursuing the calling you have placed on my life. Your word says our words have power and that life and death lies in the power of the tongue. I ask that you help me to speak life over every promise and plan you have spoken over me. I declare today that I am blessed, my businesses are blessed, and I am a blessing to others. In Jesus' name, Amen.*

## Reflection and Reaction

What excuses have you used to hinder you? Examine outside influences.

What inner voices, thoughts, etc. have you allowed to hinder you? Get rid of inner defilement.

Write your own "I Am" statement to help begin to eliminate inner defilement.

________________________________________________

________________________________________________

________________________________________________

________________________________________________

________________________________________________

# 80

# The People Are Hungry

*I have compassion on the multitude, because they have now continued with Me three days and have nothing to eat. And if I send them away hungry to their own houses, they will faint on the way; for some of them have come from afar."*

*Mark 8: 2-3*

*His Lord said to him, 'Well done good and faithful servant; you were faithful over a few things, I will make you ruler over many things. Enter into the joy of your Lord.'*

*Matthew 25: 21*

I am a stickler for excellent customer service. Customer service is a big determinate of my loyalty. I will pay the max of what I can afford for good customer service. While sitting watching TV, I see commercial after commercial advertising deals, discounts, and specials for new customers. In my mind, I ask well what about the existing customers? Do we not deserve a deal, discount or special for our loyalty? Are we not worth a marketing plan to keep us happy? Do they not understand the power of reviews?

As I continued to contemplate my questions in my head. I heard God say, "But you are doing the same thing." As entrepreneurs we complain about the lack of support, lack of followers, lack of customers, complaints over the cost and quality of our products while neglecting those who are loyal. As an author I complained about those not reading my books, not following me on social media, not writing reviews, or not buying my books. What about those who have? What about the few who are in your corner, who took a chance on a new product/business, or who sing your praises? Do they not deserve your attention, time and commitment? Jesus taught those who followed Him, he did not worry or complain about those who didn't.

The people are hungry. Are you going to continue to let them leave without being fed? They have been with you from the beginning. They believed in you. Continuing to ignore them has left them unable to speak. They can't talk about food they're not getting. Feed the flock you have. As they receive nourishment they will tell others. In fact don't even place your faith in word of mouth. Be faithful over the few and watch God increase you. Character, commitment, hard-work, determination, persistence, are noticed and will draw others to you. Don't get caught up in the numbers, let the numbers catch you. Our job is obedience, the results are up to God.

**PRAYER:** *Most gracious and precious Lord, forgive me for being distracted by numbers. Help me to remember that it is not about me but about winning souls for the kingdom and glorifying you in all that I do. As I wait for you to enlarge my territory and prepare me for your platform I thank you for teaching me integrity in handling the few that you have already given me. Continue to bless the work of my hands and guide me on the path of righteousness for your name sake. In Jesus' name, Amen.*

## Reflection and Reaction

Don't let them or it starve!

Are you neglecting the customers you have, seeking new ones?

Are you neglecting the job you have, seeking a new one?

Don't trample over the blessings you have trying to obtain the ones you don't. Learn to take care of what and who you have and watch God give the increase.

_______________________________________________

_______________________________________________

_______________________________________________

_______________________________________________

_______________________________________________

_______________________________________________

_______________________________________________

_______________________________________________

_______________________________________________

# 81

# Protect the Gift

*He said to them, "But who do you say that I am?" Peter answered and said to Him, "You are the Christ." Then He strictly warned them that they should tell no one about Him. And He began to teach them that the Son of Man must suffer many things, and be rejected by the elders and chief priests and scribes, and be killed, and after three days rise again. He spoke this word openly. Then Peter took Him aside and began to rebuke Him. But when He had turned around and looked at His disciples, He rebuked Peter, saying "Get behind Me, Satan! For you are not mindful of the things of God, but the things of men."*

*Mark 8: 29-33*

Peter said in one minute "You are the Christ," and the next he was rebuking Him. We know that Peter spoke out of love and compassion. After all no one wants to hear about the death of a loved one, especially one so violent. People can know who you are without understanding your assignment. Meaning they can know your gift but not know how God will use it.

God reveals on a need to know basis. The dream was spoken to you. The assignment was given to you. The instructions were laid out to you. It is your job to protect it from manipulators, abusers, users and murderers. And yes you must also protect it from those who are ignorant of its power and use. Peter did not know the power of the words he spoke. He did not know what it truly meant when He called Jesus the Christ. Such ignorance could have been a catastrophe and altered the course of our salvation had Jesus allowed him to speak against what God had already said.

For example, Tylenol is intended as a pain reliever. However in the hands of an infant it could cause death due to the dosage and the potential for accidental overuse. Therefore to protect those who are not able to read labels, the pills are packaged in a tamper proof container making it difficult to open by children. Not everyone is equipped to read your label. Not everyone needs or is ready to handle what you have at this very moment.

Protect the gift. Be careful of what you say in casual conversation. Be careful what you disclose on social media. Every step you take or are going to take in the future should not be broadcasted. Doing so opens the door to criticism, misunderstanding, misinterpretation, stealing of ideas, and also gives the enemy a point of attack. In our excitement we are quick to share what the Lord is doing, but we must have discernment and practice discretion in knowing when to share.

Share the testimony not the strategy. Your testimony glorifies God. Strategy seeks self-gratification and praise. Strategy is only to be revealed at the completion of the process. God is strategic in revealing certain parts of His plan for our lives to us, why then are we so loose in revealing it to others? No one can confirm what God has commanded for your life. Likewise no one can curse what God has blessed.

**PRAYER:** *Dear Lord, thank you for the gifts you have placed in me. I ask for your forgiveness in allowing my left hand to see what my right hand is doing. Help me to remember that all that I do is for your glory and not for power and esteem from others. Your word says promotion comes from you and I thank you that in your perfect timing every promise that you have spoken shall come to pass. Help me to be patient and adhere to the specific instructions you have given me. In Jesus' name, Amen.*

## Reflection and Reaction

Are you vulnerable to attack?

Do you reveal every step of God's plan to whomever will listen? How can you practice discretion?

Do you allow others to speak against what you know God has spoken? What actions can you take to protect the gift?

______________________________________________

______________________________________________

______________________________________________

______________________________________________

______________________________________________

______________________________________________

# 82

# For Christ's Sake

*So Jesus answered and said, "Assuredly, I say to you, there is no one who has left house or brothers or sisters or fathers or mother or wife or children or lands for my sake and the gospel's, who shall not receive a hundredfold now in this time – houses and brothers and sisters and mothers and children and lands, with persecutions – and in the age to come eternal life.*

*Mark 10: 29-30*

Have you ever asked God "Why the need for the solitude?" on the journey to fulfill purpose. Often times you are left with no support from family or friends and it's even difficult to gain new support. At a time when you are still trying to convince yourself, encourage yourself and understand your assignment; God will separate you from others. I am reminded of how God dealt with His disciples. When He spoke to the multitudes He spoke in parables, but when He was alone with His disciples He revealed the mysteries of the kingdom.

The separation is not punishment. The separation is in preparation of the difficult times ahead. God has to be alone with you that He may reveal to you the mysteries of the kingdom, your platform and your territory. He cannot send you out unprepared. Lack of preparation presents an open door to the enemy. Lack of preparation presumes weakness. If you are still seeking to understand, you must wait until you fully understand. If you are still seeking support, you must wait until you realize God is all you need. If you are still trying to convince yourself, you must wait until you have faith that God's choice is perfect. If you are still needing to encourage and motivate yourself, you must wait until your Yes is unwavering.

Anything that you give up and anyone that you walk away from, for Christ's sake, will be given back to you one hundredfold. However you must have the courage to walk away first. You must be brave enough to go, in spite of, and in the face of fear. Many look for the replacement first. They want new friends before they let go of the old. A new beau before they walk away from the current one. A new job before they quit the old one. Regardless of how unhappy they are or how much they complain about the old. The world has conditioned us to sacrifice obedience for perception. When God instructs us to remove people and things from our lives, we must learn to stop holding on.

Learn to let go and not mourn the loss. The time spent mourning prolongs the arrival of the new. But don't be deceived, there will be persecution (hostility and ill-treatment). But it is better to go through the persecution with God than to go through without Him. Remember that not all the people and things that God removes will be bad, they or it may just not be good for your assignment.

**PRAYER:** *Lord I thank you for choosing me. I thank you for the assignment and purpose on my life. Give me the strength to heed your command and walk away from things and people that hinder my growth in you. Give me discernment to recognize those that are for me and those that are against me. Your word says that if I draw nigh to you, you will draw nigh to me. Your word also says that if I abide in you, you will abide in me. I thank you that I can have peace in knowing that your will is what's best for me and you know what you are doing. Help my unbelief. In Jesus' name, Amen.*

## Reflection and Reaction

Are you willing to give up people and things for Christ's sake, for your purpose?

Do you complain about the separation, being alone or those who turned their backs?

You must give it up in order to get the double-fold return. Remember God is with you and He promised to provide all your needs.

# 83

# The Lord Has Need of It

*Now when they drew near Jerusalem, to Bethphage and Bethany, at the Mount of Olives, He sent two of His disciples; and He said to them, "Go into the village opposite you; and as soon as you have entered it you will find a colt tied, on which no one has sat. Loose it and bring it. And if anyone says to you, "Why are you doing this?" say, "The Lord has need of it," and immediately he will send it here." So they went their way and found the colt tied by the door outside on the street, and they loosed it. But some of those who stood there said to them, "what are you doing, loosing the colt?" And they spoke to them just as Jesus had commanded. So they let them go.*

*Mark 11: 1-6*

There will come a time in this journey in which the Lord will ask you to do something that makes no logical sense. It will appear crazy and unpopular. It will require complete trust and faith. It will require you to look fear, opposition, and even peers right in the face and declare thus said the Lord! It will require immediate decision and movement. Failure to act quickly, wasting time, can cause you to miss the move of God.

Failure to follow instructions can also cause problems. Sometimes it's not what you do or how you do it. Sometimes it's about who you do it for. There is power in Jesus' name. There are people who still reverence and respect His name. There are people who have an intimate relationship with Him and are living according to His instruction.

The Lord has prepared the way. He has the journey already set. He has prepared and spoken to the hearts of the people you will encounter along the way. But you must speak and do as He instructed. Again we see the importance of communication. When God sent Moses, He instructed him to say "I am that I am" sent him. Now He is telling the disciples to say "The Lord has need of it." You are not going on your own accord but it is He who sent you, it is He who has need of you that has the power.

The door will not open, if you don't have the right key. This is why our way doesn't work. Our name has no power or influence. Our name has no reputation of grace, mercy, or compassion. Our name has no healing or saving power. Our efforts and commands do not put angels to flight. But it is His name that carries all glory and all power. It is His voice that causes heaven to stand at attention and angels to leap. When people ask what you are doing. When people ask why you are doing it. Proclaim the name of the Lord and watch doors open and even your enemies will step aside. It is His name that sustains, keeps, and guides you, not your own works. Brag on

God, not on yourself. Wait for His instructions and do exactly as told. The Lord has need of you.

**PRAYER:** *Dear God, I admit that I am afraid. I admit that fear has caused me to doubt your voice and procrastinate on your instructions. I ask that you help me to move and do in spite of fear. Help me to trust that your way is better than my way. Help me to remember that you are always with me and that your word will never lead me where your grace can not cover me. Thank you for your Holy Spirit by whose indwelling I am able to do exactly what you called me to do. In Jesus' name, Amen.*

**Reflection and Reaction**

Not in your own strength, but in the name of Jesus, shall doors begin to open.

Do you feel your work is in vain?

Are you frustrated people don't know you, understand you, or recognize your gifts and talents?

Let go and let God be your mouthpiece!

___

___

___

___

___

___

___

___

___

# 84

# Believe That You Receive, Do Not Doubt

*So Jesus answered and said to them, "Have faith in God. For assuredly, I say to you, whoever says to this mountain, 'Be removed and be cast into the sea,' and does not doubt in his heart, but believes that those things he says will be done, he will have whatever he says. Therefore I say to you, whatever things you ask when you pray, believe that you receive them, and you will have them."*

*Mark 11: 22-24*

Have faith. Two little and simple words with such powerful meaning. What is faith? People tell you to have it, but few can explain how you know you got it. Faith simply means assurance in God. It requires complete surrender and absolute trust. It requires sacrifice of human thinking and emotions for the pure word of God. You must take on a "regardless of what it looks like or what people say, if God said it, it will come to pass" attitude. It requires protection of God's word at all costs, as many will come to manipulate, interrogate and falsely translate that very word. It requires a "not easily offended, throw your best shot" way of living. Why? Because faith will be tested. But rest assured, each test is preparing you for a greater platform, an enlarged territory, and the increase that you prayed for.

Do not doubt. Three little words, yet so heavily weighted. What is doubt? What does it look like? It is a feeling, a temporary lapse in judgement, a sudden influx of fear that infiltrates our minds at the break of a great manifestation of God's promises. As the old saints once said, "when the devil starts fighting hard, your breakthrough is closer than you think." Doubt comes when we reach crossroads and turning points in our lives. When it's time to put up or shut up, here comes doubt. Doubt comes in the form of uncertainty, lack of conviction, unsureness, indecision, hesitation, suspicion, confusion, questioning, insecurity, skepticism, and distrust. Contemplating something over and over in your mind, is a form of doubt. The book of proverbs states a double-minded man is unstable in all his ways and can obtain nothing from the Lord. Doubt is the root of double-mindedness. God is not fickle. His word, His command, and His instructions are clear and precise.

To doubt yourself is to doubt the God in you! God is not a magician, He works through people…mainly YOU! He can't do anything in your life without your participation. He is a gentleman, He will not force His plan on you. You must invite Him and allow Him control. You halt his hand when you doubt your abilities, your gifts, and your talents, you doubt His call, His choice, and His plan. He knows who you are, He knows what you can do yet He still chose you. Accept His choice, accept the call and allow Him to show Himself strong through you. For in your weakness, He is made strong. You can do this because He that is in you, the author and finisher of your faith, can do the impossible!

**PRAYER:** *Dear God. Forgive me for doubting the gifts and talents you have placed in me and thus preventing your ability to use me for your kingdom. Forgive me for allowing doubt to cause fear and preventing me from completely surrendering to your will. I acknowledge that I am nothing without you. I thank you for the anointing you have on my life. I thank you for strengthening me to do your will. Help me to surrender to you daily and to reverence you in all my ways. I thank you that I am your sheep and I know your voice. I believe that I will receive all that I have prayed for and will walk in faith not by sight. In Jesus' name, Amen.*

## Reflection and Reaction

What area are you most doubtful about?

What does the word say? Find scriptures that strengthen you to meditate on day and night.

Remember God's choice is perfect and you are perfect for the job.

____________________________________________________________

____________________________________________________________

# 85

# Watch and Pray

*Then He came and found them sleeping, and said to Peter, "Simon, are you sleeping? Could you not watch one hour? Watch and pray, lest you enter into temptation. The spirit indeed is willing, but the flesh is weak."*

*Mark 14: 37-38*

No wonder the disciples were confused. Jesus could be talking about the current situation one minute and flip to the future the next. When He asked Peter could he not watch one hour, I believe he was speaking of him watching for those coming to take Him and perhaps deliver Him before His time. But in the very next verse He said "watch and pray, lest you enter into temptation." We are to watch for those coming and seeking to betray Jesus and His word over our life. We are to watch for those seeking to destroy God's plan, manipulate the word, confuse you, frustrate you and cancel your assignment. Watch for those that come to distract you from your goals. How do we watch? We pray.

We assume that this journey will be one of happiness and joy. But God's way will eventually lead you into the darkness, into the wilderness to be tested. A place so dark that you will become weary. So weary that you will not have the strength to turn on or even search for the light. Rather you will find yourself crawling on the floor, curling up in a corner, and crying yourself to sleep. But through prayer, you will find that in that very moment, the peace of God is there with you, has wrapped His arms around you, and is shielding you from the dangers that lurk in the darkness. As you sleep, as you rest, God is strengthening you for the next point in the journey, giving you the ability to wake up and cut on the light.

Prayer keeps communication open between you and God. It does not prevent darkness, rather it opens your spiritual eyes that you may see the enemy lurking. That you may know that good opportunity is not His will though it seems good. That you may see that your best friend does not have your best interest at heart. That you may see that your church member is plotting to take your place. That you may see that the enemy seeks to devour you through loneliness and fear. Prayer is your shield in the midst of warfare. Failure to pray is waving the flag of surrender to the enemy. Failure to pray is getting weary in well-doing. Failure to pray is succumbing to temptation. Failure to pray is admitting defeat. Failure to pray is shutting the door to the blessings and promises of God. Failure to pray is accepting mediocrity and yielding to conquest. Watch and Pray, that you may be strengthened, that you may be enlightened, that you may be filled with wisdom, that you may have discernment, and that you may be more that a conqueror. The victory is yours. The Promised Land is yours. You must remain in His presence which is only obtained through consistent communication, commonly known as prayer.

**PRAYER:** *Dear God, Forgive me for allowing the cares of life and this world to distract me from communicating with you and basking in your presence. I thank you for your rod of correction, as your word says you chastise those you love. Thank you for loving me and thank you for showing me how to protect and nurture the gifts you have placed in me. Continue to lead and guide me into all truths. Continue to order my footsteps. I acknowledge you in all my ways and ask that you help me to delight in you daily through prayer. In Jesus' name, Amen.*

**<u>Reflection and Reaction</u>**

Have you allowed busyness to prevent you from praying?

How many days this week did you pray? How did your missed prayer time affect your day or open the door for the enemy?

Incorporate more time with God into your daily life and watch Him work out whatever concerns you.

______________________________________________

______________________________________________

# 86

# But the Scriptures Must Be Fulfilled

*Then Jesus answered and said to them, "Have you come out, as against a robber, with swords and clubs to take Me? I was daily with you in the temple teaching, and you did not seize Me. But the scriptures must be fulfilled." Then they all forsook Him and fled.*

*Mark 14: 48-50*

The attack of the enemy is calculated. He has great patience and will use more than one person to come against you. Remember our friend Job. Satan was going to and fro seeking whom He could devour. He showed up in heaven. God offered Job to Him, He asked "Have you considered my servant Job?" Satan's response was that God had a hedge of protection around him. God responded, you can touch anything he has, only do not take his life. Satan's whole purpose was to get Job to curse God. We know the story, we know Job stood strong. We know He received double for his trouble in the end.

What we tend to forget is that Satan's plan of attack was carefully orchestrated. He did not kill his animals and stop. He kept getting stronger and stronger. One attack after another, and Job still did not curse his God. The same is happening here. Throughout Jesus' ministry the enemy was sending people, Pharisees and scribes, to question everything He was doing. Jesus did not bend. The scriptures had to be fulfilled. The enemy sent demons to test Him, to foretell of who He was and His coming, Jesus cast them out and still did not bend, the scriptures had to be foretold. Now he sent robbers with swords and clubs. Jesus let them know, I see you devil, you had plenty of opportunity to do what you wanted to do, but yet you go get a whole army for little ole me (my interpretation)…..but the scriptures must be fulfilled.

In other words, regardless of what you throw at me, God's word will prevail, it is going to happen just the way He planned it. In fact the enemy don't even recognize he part of the plan. The enemy thinks he is using people to destroy Jesus when God is using him to bring salvation to the world. As with you, the enemy thinks he is using people to attack you and prevent you from doing the work of the Lord, when God is using him to produce a greater work in you and glorify His name.

Don't be ashamed or take offense that people leave or left during your time of trouble. It was not meant for them to be there. If they are there, if they assist you, then they can take credit for your coming out, your victory, your testimony. Trouble has a way of separating the wheat from the tares, the strong from the weak. Only the strong can survive the storm. But the storm must come in order to make the weak visible. Count it all joy that God chose you to whether the storm. He knows what He put in you. He has confidence that you will make it. The scriptures must be fulfilled, His word will not return to Him void. The enemy will be defeated, you will be victorious, if you faint not!

**PRAYER:** *Dear Heavenly Father, your word states to give thanks in all things. Though I am in the storm right now, I thank you that you are with me and I am victorious. Help me to place all my cares on you and to not focus on who stays and who goes but rather the word being fulfilled in my life. In Jesus' name, Amen.*

## Reflection and Reaction

Has the pain become unbearable? Does the test seem too hard? Do you feel you are taking on more than you can bear?

There is a test to get to the testimony.

There is a process to get to the promise.

Don't give up during the test, don't abort the process.

Keep your eyes on the promise. God will remember your pain. He will remember your tears.

# 87

# Self-Preservation Proceeds Denial

*Now as Peter was below in the courtyard, one of the servant girls of the high priest came. And when she saw Peter warming himself, she looked at him and said, "You also were with Jesus of Nazareth." But he denied it saying "I neither know nor understand what you are saying." And he went out on the porch, and a rooster crowed. And the servant girl say him again, and began to say to those who stood by, "This is one of them." But he denied it again. And a little later those who stood by said to Peter again, 'Surely you are one of them; for you are a Galilean, and your speech shows it." Then he began to curse and swear, "I do not know this Man of who you speak!" A second time the rooster crowed. Then Peter called to mind the word that Jesus had said to him, "Before the rooster crows twice, you will deny Me three times." And when he thought about it, he wept.*

*Mark 14: 66-72*

Either Peter was hard of hearing, or he was not paying attention when the rooster crowed the first time. There was some time, though we don't know how much, between the first and third denial as well as between the first and second crow. He actually had time to get it right. He had time to decide to put it all on the line and claim the goodness of the one he had been following for months. Yet he did not recognize the warning. Though you would think a rooster crowing would jog your memory. But Peter is no different from us. We can be caught up in our own selves, our own issues, and our own well-being that we fail to heed God's warning.

Self-preservation can cause you to deny the very God you serve. We go to church every Sunday, then go to work and are gossipers and mess starters on the job. We teach bible study or lead a ministry, yet cheat on our taxes. We know God is calling us to fulltime ministry, yet we refuse to leave our jobs. Why? Fear that it may not work out, or fear we will lose our independence or the money we have become accustomed to. But who are we really fooling? We walk with Jesus. We look like him. We talk like him. Yet when it comes time to allow the word to prevail in our lives we deny the very God we proclaim to serve. And like Peter, when we have exhausted all possibilities, when we are tired of running, and when we realize that what we were trying to preserve is miniscule to what we could have gained…we weep.

One minute we proclaim to love the Lord and would do anything to please him, but the moment we are asked to sacrifice our homes, our jobs, our plans for success, we turn our backs and walk away with our heads bowed in defeat. Did you not read your bible? Do you not recall the many brave men and women in the bible who risked it all to follow Jesus and the great rewards and legacies they left behind? As believers we are descendants of Abraham and partakers of his inheritance.

Yet we still doubt Him? We still question the call he has placed on our lives. Dare to trust him. Dare to step out on faith. Dare to move according to His word. Don't allow fear and self-preservation to cause you to miss the hand of God and leave you with a life time of regret. Yes it will be hard and yes there will be tears. It is better that you weep now and await your joy in the morning that to weep later on the day of judgment when asked what you did with the talents He gave you. God is a rewarder of those who trust Him. Anything that you lose for His sake, He has to repay.

**PRAYER:** *Dear Heavenly Father, I admit that the call you have placed on my life has caused a great deal of fear. However your word instructs me to not be afraid. I thank you that you are with me everywhere I go and you can do all things but fail. I release my fears of inadequacy, failure, and disappointment into your hands. And replace them with confidence, trust, and belief that you will complete the work you begun in me and equip me for the call. In Jesus' name, Amen.*

## Reflection and Reaction

The rooster is crowing!

Are you going to proclaim Jesus and boldly accept the call on your life or will you continue to deny him?

To accept Jesus you must accept all of Him, not just bits and pieces, or what is comfortable for you.

___

___

___

___

# 88

# Silence During Accusation

*And the chief priests accused Him of many things, but He answered nothing. Then Pilate asked Him again, saying "Do You answer nothing? See how many things they testify against You!" But Jesus still answered nothing so that Pilate marveled.*

*Mark 15: 3-5*

It does not feel good when you are attacked. It does not feel good when the very people that claimed to love you one minute are conspiring with the enemy to harm and destroy you in the next minute. It certainly does not feel good when you know that you have done nothing wrong, when you know you have been falsely accused, when you know, that they know you know, it's a lie and yet the Holy Spirit within you instructs you to say nothing.

There is no hurt like a hurt that cannot be defended. Harsh words or abuse from family or an authority figure, leave lifetime scars. Why? Because these people were supposed to protect you from harm, instead they inflicted the harm, and due to their role of authority you had to hold it all inside. Defense allows us to protect our heart. But Jesus showed us another way. You don't have to defend you. You don't have to protect your heart. God will do it for you. And in doing so, you will bring blessings to all those who come behind you. Jesus reminded us, that the temporary trial, the temporary hurt, and the temporary accusations, had a far greater reward.

Silence during accusation is more bewildering to the accuser. They can't understand why you, of the same human nature as them, refuse to defend yourself. What is it about you that makes you different? Why are you not affected by their best shot? When we say yes to the will of God, we also say yes to the persecution, knowing regardless of what happens we will be victorious. When we resist the urge to defend ourselves, and choose to remain silent, we enact the power of God to work on our behalf. When we are silent, we enable God to speak and to do what He intended to do. The enemy is marveled.

Silence during accusation allows you to hear God. When you are commissioned to do a work for the Lord, it is not you they are accusing but rather He who sent you. It is not you they are hurting, but rather He who sent you. It is not you they are refusing to receive or acknowledge, but rather He who sent you. Therefore He who sent you, is obligated to defend you. We have to trust that whether God decides to intervene and remove you from the fire now or later, He is able and His plan is best. So let them talk about you. Let them conjure up false allegations against you. Let them attack your integrity. Remember it is not you they are attacking, but the God in you. You are covered. You will get the victory. All things will work out for your good in the end. Continue to hold your head up. Continue to do what God called you to do. The enemies, the naysayers, the doubters, the gossipers, are God's problem. Hold your peace and let the Lord fight your battles.

**PRAYER:** *Dear God thank you for being my shield. I thank you for your blood covering over my life and all that I put my hands to do. Help me to remember that though I walk through the valley of the shadow of death I shall fear no evil. You are my protection. You are my strong tower. In you I put my trust and of no man shall I be afraid. In Jesus' name, Amen.*

## Reflection and Reaction

Are you struggling to hold you peace?

Are you struggling to find your happy place?

Don't do it in your own strength, let God do it for you? Ask Him to reveal your physical hiding place. Take a walk, find a new hobby, meditate, etc. Do whatever you need to do to escape and remain silent. Sit back and watch the Lord do His thing!

________________________________________________

________________________________________________

# 89

# Condemnation Only Exists in Unbelief

*And He said to them, "Go into all the world and preach the gospel to every creature. He who believes and is baptized will be saved; but he who does not believe will be condemned."*

*Mark 16: 15-16*

Salvation is free but it requires your belief. What does it mean to believe? Belief is defined as "surety that God is capable of a particular action." Christians confuse capable with obligation. Capable means that he is able to do it, not that He is required to. Therefore belief is an everyday "But God."

It don't look like it..."But God."

It don't feel like it..."But God."

I don't understand... "But God."

I don't know how... "But God."

Time is the biggest hindrance to belief. Things don't happen as fast as or when we think they should. Belief believes that God can, regardless of time and God will, right on time. Belief rejects frustration, doubt, and naysayers in the wait. Belief does not mean that those things don't come. It just means belief does not let them in the house when they do. As long as you proclaim to be a servant of the Lord, the enemy is either at war with you or planning an attack against you. He only leaves for a time or season.

Condemnation only exists in unbelief. In God there is love, forgiveness, peace, joy and salvation. Without belief in Him these things cannot exist. This lack of existence welcomes in the spirit of condemnation. Searching for love, punishment, unrest, sadness, eternal damnation all plague a heart that does not believe. Belief stands on the word of God. Has God promised you something? Find the scripture that coincides with that word, write it down, proclaim it in prayer, meditate on it, and watch God perform it. And when the enemy begins to attack, proclaim the word. "Get behind me Satan" does not work if it is not proceeded with "It is written..."

Condemnation specializes in defeat. But belief teaches us how to fight. Each attack of the enemy is different, belief keeps us on our toes that we are not overpowered. Believe in God today. No matter how hard or how impossible His promises may seem, believe His word. Stand and when you have done all else stand some more. God will not allow you to fail, he will not allow His word to return to Him void. He cannot lie. His word must perform what it set out to do. God cannot move in your life through unbelief. If things are not happening, check your belief system. Repent and watch God.

**PRAYER:** *Dear God, forgive me for not believing in your word. Forgive me for allowing condemnation to harden my heart towards your promises. Thank you for your forgiveness and I ask you to help my unbelief, help me to trust you, help me to walk by faith and not by sight. Help me to intensify my relationship with you because I know that the more I know you the more I will trust and believe you. Thank you for your patience and lovingkindness towards me. In Jesus' name, Amen.*

**Reflection and Reaction**

Are things stagnant in your life? Do you feel stuck?

Check your belief system. Do your thoughts and actions coincide with what you are believing?

What are you believing God for? What are you saying about it vocally or subconsciously?

____________________________________________________________

____________________________________________________________

____________________________________________________________

____________________________________________________________

# 90

# Awaken the Dream

*For I know the thoughts that I think toward you, says the Lord, thoughts of peace and not of evil, to give you a future and a hope. Then you will call upon Me and go and pray to Me, and I will listen to you. And you will seek Me and find Me, when you search for Me with all your heart. I will be found by you says the Lord, and I will bring you back from your captivity; I will gather you from all the nations and from all the places where I have driven you, says the Lord, and I will bring you to the place from which I cause you to be carried away captive.*

*Jeremiah 29: 11-14*

God loves you. I know we hear this often, but you need to really get this down in your spirit. GOD LOVES YOU! If you do not comprehend or understand this, you will be unable to pursue the dream that He has placed inside of you. His love is unconditional. Nothing you did, have done or could do can make Him stop loving you. GOD LOVES YOU. Have no regrets. There are no mistakes. The past, regardless of how bad it was, regardless of what you thought you were missing, regardless of what you didn't do, regardless of the decisions you made, regardless of who hurt, abused or misused you, and regardless of who you hurt, abused or misused, does not remove you from His love. No matter what the past looks like, IT WAS NOT A MISTAKE!

Even when you thought you messed up, it was all part of the plan. God is like a GPS system in that, regardless of what turn you make, or what road you take, you will eventually end up at your final destination. Every turn, every road, makes the journey more interesting. What you thought was a mistake, was a necessary ingredient to help prepare you for God's use. Don't stay stuck in the mistake. Don't allow the enemy to consume you with thoughts of should have, could have or would have. The sooner you hand it over to God, the quicker He can show you how He wants to use it for your good. Remember God already knows, it's the revelation to you that slows the process.

Awaken the dream. You can't out dream God. In fact you probably aren't dreaming big enough! In addition, what you are dreaming about now is only a small portion of what God has for you. Why? Because as you go, as you submit to His will, as you hear His voice and obey His command, more opportunities will become available and your dream will expand. With God, as you develop a relationship with Him the impossible becomes the possible and opens your worldview.

Awaken the dream. Just start today. If you are unhappy. If things aren't going right. I want you to do two things. First set a time for prayer and meet God there every day. Second spend some time each day doing something that makes you happy, whether it is picking up a hobby or planning that business you have always dreamed of. The key is to get started and God will match you efforts. Life is too short to be unhappy and live in mediocrity. You have the power to change it. He lives inside of you and He loves you so much and is waiting for you to ask for His help. It's not as hard as you think. No one becomes a business owner, millionaire, author, etc. overnight. One day at a time, step by step makes any dream a reality.

Awaken the dream. You owe it to yourself. You owe it to your children. You owe it to your family. You owe it to the world. Aren't you curious? What if you fail? But what if you succeed? If you don't try, failure is guaranteed. Remember there is no failure in God only lessons to be learned. Learn the lesson, apply the principle and move on. Stop beating yourself up. You are exactly where God wants you to be. Your dream is available to you now. All you have to do is say yes and allow God to open the door to endless possibilities.

**PRAYER:** *Dear God, I know you created me for a purpose. I know that your thoughts toward me are of peace, hope and an expected future. I relinquish to you all that I am past, present and future and submit to your will for my life. Your word says all things work for the good of those who love the Lord and I patiently wait to see how you will utilize all that has transpired in my life. Open my spiritual eyes, reveal to me the purpose you have for my life and lead me on the path to obtain all that I desire and all that you have for me. Thank you for choosing me to be a light unto this world. In Jesus' name, Amen.*

## Reflection and Reaction

Are you ready for the life you always wanted?

Are you sick and tired of being sick and tired?

Dream Big! Think Big! Look up to the hills from which cometh your help.

All you need is the first step!

What in your past consumes you with thoughts of unworthiness and inadequacy? Give it to God, so that He can use it for your good.

Made in the USA
San Bernardino, CA
10 February 2017